ELIZABETH CLEMANTS

HEALING TOGETHER

A Family Guide TO RECOVERING FROM SEXUAL HARM

APRIL 2025

DEDICATED TO

THE HIDDEN WATER COMMUNITY
PAST - PRESENT AND FUTURE

TABLE OF CONTENTS

ABOUT THIS BOOK

In the Summer of 2015, I found myself on the roof of a rented house in San Miguel de Allende, Mexico. I could hear my three young children playing below in the internal courtyard. My niece Taylor, a recent college graduate who was working for me at the time, sat at the dining room table answering emails. After years of struggle, my divorce was nearly final. Looking out over that old city, I kept turning over in my mind: where do I go from here?

The answer came immediately: Write the book about Hidden Water.

This response caught me off guard. Hidden Water was still in its infancy, more concept than reality. I had lots of other work I was already doing, and a family to support. Yet the certainty I felt of this direction was undeniable. I knew that to write this book Hidden Water itself would need to grow beyond its current ideological potential into something real. The full scope of the work, and therefore the wisdom, was yet to unfold.

When I had gone up to the roof, I had told Taylor I was going to sit there and figure out my life. She laughed, "Ah, good luck with that. I guess that means I will be making dinner," not even looking up from her computer. I was back in minutes. Taylor looked at me as she got up to make herself a tea and said, "That was fast. You figured out your whole life already?" Full of inspiration, I answered, "Yes, I think I did."

Together we refocused our work efforts on developing the structure that is now Hidden Water: An organization dedicated to a restorative justice familial response to sexual harm of young people. That moment sparked a convergence of all my work in conflict resolution, shamanic healing, and social work, blending restorative justice principles and ancient indigenous circle practices to create something innovative for families. Looking back, I see how sitting on that roof made this book the driving force that created what Hidden Water is today. I have spent more than a decade working on the book and building the organization, each informing the other in important ways.

By the Winter of 2016, I was standing before our first healing circle, surrounded by nine of my friends who had also experienced sexual harm in their youth. As I gripped the talking piece, getting ready to speak the first words in this very first circle, my intellectual mind stepped aside, and it struck me I would have to face my own sexual harm. The revelation stunned me. Looking back, I wonder if I had unconsciously avoided this realization; perhaps knowing on some level that confronting my own pain might have stopped me from creating this work altogether.

For years I had guided others toward healing while keeping my own trauma at arm's length. The sexual harm I endured from my godfather and others sat neatly categorized in my mind, intellectually processed but emotionally untouched. Now, standing before these women, I knew I could no longer maintain that distance. The work I had created demanded my full participation—not just as a leader, but as someone who also needed to heal.

Looking back, I understand how this distancing protected me, letting me build a life despite the harm. There, in that circle of friends who carried similar wounds, I knew I had to let down a wall and let myself be seen. Not intellectually, nor to help others but for myself. I reached for what I'd stored away on that high dusty shelf in my mind and started to speak.

This wasn't just about naming past trauma as I had done for years in private therapy. It was about openly embodying the harm, acknowledging the impact and sharing it in a community of others who could relate and bear witness. It is a privilege to share here what I and others have learned through this journey.

The approach we developed which is outlined in these pages is interdisciplinary. It draws from social work concepts, conflict resolution theory, a family systems lens, a restorative justice worldview and the personal experiences of those impacted by sexual abuse. Through this combined perspective, we honor both the intricate web of family bonds and each person's sovereign journey toward healing. While every path is distinct, this book seeks to offer companionship along the way, illuminating possibilities without prescribing solutions. The hope is we are able to catalyze healing that can transform families for generations.

Thank you for joining me in creating this change in the world.

—ELIZABETH

AUTHOR'S NOTE

This book offers a perspective on child sexual abuse that extends beyond what many readers may expect. Instead of focusing solely on the victim's experience, this book examines the broader impact on family systems. This wider lens is not meant to minimize the devastating impact of sexual harm on victims. Rather, my hope is to provide a framework for understanding how families can navigate the aftermath of harm, how the larger system is also negatively impacted, and what healing can look like across generations. This paradigm shift is meant to augment prevention as well as take the entire burden of healing off of the victim.

There are two givens in this work that seem important to share upfront. First, sexual harm invariably impacts the victim negatively, regardless of circumstances. The nature and depth of this impact is unique to each individual and exists independently of the offending person's intentions, good qualities or individual circumstances. When someone identifies an experience as harmful, that reality stands on its own merit. Families are not courtrooms; we need not engage in proving or litigating these experiences.

Second, there is an intrinsic humanity in all people involved in the sexual harm. This level of worth can not be altered, added to through good deeds or subtracted from by bad ones. While all people do not behave in ways that foster safety in the world for others, we strive in this work to hold us all accountable for our actions while holding tight to each person's intrinsic worth.

Rather than categorizing people as 'good' or 'bad,' we consider whether or not someone is willing to engage in the necessary work of healing and who is not yet ready to do so. This book moves beyond binary frameworks of guilty versus innocent. While the primary and most profound impact falls on the victim, understanding sexual harm requires everyone involved to examine how they have been impacted, how they are impacting others, and how they want to show up in their important relationships now.

There are four research-based understandings that shape this work:

- **Over 90% of sexual harm to young people is committed by someone known to the victim, often a family member or someone close to the family.**
- **At least 50% of such harm is committed by other young people, who rarely grow up to harm sexually as adults.**
- **Only 12% of abuse situations are reported to authorities.**
- **On average, it takes 25 years for a victim to disclose their sexual harm experience.**

This work addresses an underserved, and often unnoticed, population: the 88% of families where childhood sexual harm remained undisclosed or unaddressed until the victim reached adulthood. By providing insight and education about the comprehensive impact of sexual abuse, this book aims to support adult survivors while also relieving them of the exhausting burden of having to explain their needs and experiences to family members. This approach creates space for more informed, supportive family responses.

The book's framework rests on four foundational objectives:

1. **To implement a systems-based understanding of how sexual abuse impacts individual family members and, by**

extension, the entire family system.

2. **To establish supportive response patterns for all family members, including those who caused sexual harm.**

3. **To redistribute the weight of the impact of the harm, and the responsibility for healing from it, so it can be shared by the whole family and not held solely by the one who was harmed.**

4. **To introduce "The Path of Healing from Harm" as a concrete model for both healing from having been harmed and healing from having caused harm — in all the ways humans hurt one another.**

Healing Together is a practical guide for families seeking to address sexual harm without causing further emotional damage. Any family member can engage with this material, and participation is not required by the other family members. In fact, one person is enough for the family healing to begin. The process expands with each person who takes part, regardless of their role in the harm. And it always starts with just one person: you, the reader.

Healing is a personal journey, and each person must choose it for themselves. If the offender is invited to take part in the family's healing, they may walk this path alongside the survivor. If not, their accountability and growth must happen separately, with the support of other loved ones. Healing cannot be forced, nor can accountability be demanded—it must be freely chosen.

If you feel compelled to share this book with family members or loved ones, do so with an open hand. Extend the invitation, but then step back. Each person must come to this work in their own time, when they are truly ready to begin.

When we try to coerce someone else's participation, it is a sign we've lost focus on our own work. We will get off track if we believe that someone else taking prescribed steps will heal us. We all must find our own way to healing. These changes require genuine commitment that can only come from within.

Physical and emotional safety must be established before any healing work can begin. If a child remains at risk or is still exposed to someone who has harmed them, addressing that danger takes absolute precedence. Even when physical safety is a relatively low risk such as in the case of the young person now being an adult, exposure to someone who has caused harm without choice can inflict deep emotional wounds for the one harmed.

The work described here is meant for adults, not children. Young people heal best when the adults around them step up and take charge of the situation. When adults confront the abuse without hesitation, believe children unequivocally, and reinforce for them that they bear no blame, the child will do much better on their healing journey.

When adults embrace their responsibility as family leaders, even if they were unaware of the harm when it occurred, they lift an enormous burden from both children and adult survivors. This book guides adults in becoming these agents of change, creating the safety and support essential for everyone's recovery.

In this model accountability and compassion go hand in hand. Speaking to the humanity of those who have caused sexual harm does not minimize their actions or discount their impact. As a survivor, I intimately understand the lifelong devastation of sexual abuse and the fierce anger it ignites. Yet I've learned that true accountability flourishes when we recognize both the gravity of harmful actions and the possibility of transformation.

This perspective represents a radical shift from our current paradigm. The practice of shaming and isolating survivors, incarcerating those who have caused harm, and leaving other family members out of the equation perpetuates cycles of trauma and creates fertile ground for further abuse. With rates of sexual harm against young people climbing, we must forge a different way forward. Only by offering paths to genuine accountability and redemption can we encourage those at risk of causing harm to seek help before they act.

Therefore, I honor the courage it takes to confront one's harmful actions and embark on the challenging journey of change. A journey that is as challenging as it is necessary. We can not stop child sexual abuse in the future by helping victims after the fact. We must work with those at risk of harming others sexually, before they act or act again.

If we don't, we will continue down the road we are on. That said, this is a book for those who are ready for healing and repair. If one is still struggling with an impulse to harm sexually, they are not yet ready for this book. They must first seek out the support one needs to address the driving force within to act out in this way.

For those who have caused sexual harm as adults, recovery involves far more than simply promising not to offend again. It requires a genuine commitment to personal growth, supported by professional guidance. Without structured support, especially during moments of vulnerability or isolation, destructive impulses can overpower even the best intentions. Building connections with others who have successfully addressed harmful behaviors is often an integral component of the recovery process. This book is a step after someone is in recovery, when our intention is to repair with others for past harm.

The landscape shifts when addressing harm caused by minors. Research confirms that most young people who engage in sexually harmful behavior do not continue this pattern into adulthood. For parents and caregivers managing problematic sexual behavior in a young person, professional support, strong boundaries and the right compassionate perspective will guide their development toward healthier sexual relationships and boundaries.

I consider the judicial system unnecessarily traumatic and counter-productive for young people under the age of twenty-five. Certainly for those under the age of 18, it can be a dangerous and highly inappropriate intervention. Young people still learning to navigate appropriate sexual boundaries benefit more from stable adult guidance and professional support when developing healthy relationship skills. Compassionate treatment, even if it must include variable limits on one's freedom, is the most effective way to prevent future harm.

The issue of sexual harm between young people in their teens and early twenties demands a nuanced understanding. While some deliberately violate consent, others may genuinely misread signals. Both scenarios harm the victim and, therefore, the impact must not be minimized. However, our response to those who caused the harm should be tailored in light of these differences.

Throughout this book, my intention is to separate the impact on the victim from the stated intention of the person who caused harm, recognizing that not all sexual harm stems from the same place in the offender or from the same understanding of the circumstances. In other words, our goal is to hold both the context of how the harm came about without minimizing the damage done to the victim.

This book intends to walk a careful line: offering an unflinching look at the healing journey while remaining accessible to those who are interested in learning. Rather than overwhelming readers with the most extreme cases of abuse, I've woven together true experiences that illuminate the complex dynamics of family harm and recovery. These composite narratives are meant to serve as bridges of understanding, showing the path forward without sensationalizing trauma. Real change requires sustained engagement, and my deepest hope is that readers will find these pages helpful and challenging but never unbearable. A text they can return to again and again as they navigate their own healing journey.

The impact of sexual harm isn't solely determined by the act itself, it's shaped by a constellation of factors: age at the time of harm, the presence or absence of safe adults, the intersection of other family trauma, availability of resources, the complexities of memory, the relationship to the offender, and access to communities beyond family walls.

Each survivor's path is further influenced by when and how they disclosed, the support they received or did not receive from loved ones, their access to outside support, and their own wellspring of resilience. As well as many other factors. We can not assume we know how sexual harm impacts an individual until they have a chance to explore that impact themselves, and speak about it to us.

This book and its healing framework are intentionally adaptable, designed to honor this diversity of experience. The path is broad enough to be relevant across many situations, and flexible enough, I hope, to meet you where you are. I recognize that not everyone has a family member willing to walk this path with them and that's okay. This book is for the individual.

Healing creates a chain reaction in an individual's environment, affecting those around them. You may be surprised to notice changes as they show up in ways or in people you didn't expect. While we can't control who in our lives will be impacted or how they'll respond, doing this work will improve your life and relationships.

As you engage with these pages I invite you to take what resonates with your personal experience and release what doesn't. Your healing journey is uniquely yours, and what may not speak to you today might be exactly what another needs to hear.

Thank you for joining me in this challenging and life-affirming conversation. We are building a new paradigm for understanding sexual harm and the possibility of healing together.

With deep compassion and hope,
Elizabeth

PART I

CHAPTER 1

Planting Seeds

The story of one of the most influential women in my life began on a humble farm in North Dakota. My grandmother lived on a homestead built by her immigrant father. She attended a one-room schoolhouse, and when she surpassed the ability of the teacher to meet her academic potential, her parents moved her to town where she could attend high school – a rare opportunity in those days for a first generation 12 year old farm girl.

She and her mother moved to Valley City, a small town miles away by wagon, while her father and brother stayed to work on the farm. Her mother opened a boarding house there, with long term tenants, and people who were just moving through. My grandmother and my great grandmother both lived and worked in the boarding house, while my grandmother also attended school. This was the opportunity that became a springboard to the rest of her amazing life.

One afternoon when I was in my thirties, I was sitting at my 95-year-old grandmother's table in her kitchen cutting strawberries. At the time I was a social worker, living and working in New York City. I loved to tell my grandmother about my work, as she was always so interested in my life. She used to say she wanted to stay alive as long as she could, just to see what I might do next. She always made me feel loved, and I felt very close to her all my life. On this day, seemingly out of nowhere, she shared this with me:

"I had the strangest memory come up yesterday," she said softly, gazing out the window as she set down her paring knife, a faraway sadness taking hold.

Midwestern folks can say the most monumental and devastating things with flat affect, as if to communicate it isn't such a big deal. Just life, matter-of-fact. Those of us who are intimately familiar with the nuance of that communication style hear more. The delivery is the plain frame for a picture that packs a punch. The pain vibrates invisibly under the subtle tones.

"I was remembering how my great uncle used to pay me a nickel if I let him put his hand in my underwear." She stopped, waiting for that to land with me.

I froze. Was I hearing what she just said? I could not fully comprehend what was happening. My heart was pounding and my hand tightened around the spoon I was no longer using to stir the cream. I couldn't bring myself to look up for a moment. The kitchen seemed to tilt around me. When I managed to lift my head, my grandmother was looking down, clearly waiting for me to say something. After an awkwardly long pause, I managed to cut through the growing silence with,

"How old were you?"

There was no hiding the contempt in my voice - not toward her, of course, but rather for the disturbing images in my mind of a child being exploited in that way. Made infinitely worse by picturing the middle-of-nowhere farm at a time when women and children had little or no recourse for such behavior. Closing my eyes, I tried to get the thought of an old man manipulating a little girl with a nickel for his own sexual satisfaction out of my mind. I just shook my head in disbelief and anger.

"Oh, probably five. But that happened more than once, so I can't be sure." My eyes widened as she averted her eyes.

I could feel my grandmother shifting from this vulnerable disclosure to that strong Scandinavian stoicism – those steel walls that carried her through her life – protecting her against these memories and maybe others like it. Her tone seemed to say: *This is just the unavoidable life of a woman, no? What can you do but just survive it?*

I thought for a minute, wondering what to say. "Did you ever tell anyone?"

I hope my words came across with the care and concern I do in fact have for her and all others who have lived through harm of this kind. But I suspect the abruptness of this disclosure caught me off guard and my questions likely came across with a tinge of accusation. It would never have been my intention to sound like I was blaming her, of course. In my confusion and a flood of feelings though, I imagine I struggled to find my footing for a loving response that communicated how sorry I was.

"No, you are the first person I have ever told. I don't even know what made me start to think about that," she said, turning away and taking another step toward shutting down this conversation.

Recalling these words makes my heart break, every time. I had been given the awesome responsibility and privilege of being a trusted confidant in that moment. I wished I had said something spectacular that would have brought about some healing, or at least a modicum of support.

Instead, I said: "What on earth would kick up a memory like that after 90 years?"

I cringe to think this is what I said, but it was. I certainly did not mean to say I wished the memory had not surfaced or that it was best left buried, but I know this was probably how it sounded. I know it is easy to say the wrong things in these moments. I wasn't trying to hurt her. I just wasn't really thinking about her with any clarity in that moment.

She shrugged, and said "I don't know. I haven't thought about it. What does it really matter? I also had sex with one of the men in the boarding house when I was 14. I certainly hated that a lot more."

As she shared about more abuse, it was as though my whole nervous system was being overloaded. My mind raced trying to go back through my whole life and understand this woman differently. Eyes widening and staring right at her as she refused to meet my gaze.

"Raped? You were raped in high school?"

At this point, my inner world was turning upside down. I recall my tone radiating from this difficult image: I did not want my beloved, wonderful grandmother to be the victim of rape. I did not know how to reconcile these horrible events with this fiery, accomplished, and intelligent woman whom I had looked up to all my life. I think I reached a point where I couldn't take it in anymore. The pain was too much for me. I can imagine it felt like I was lashing out at her.

She responded with what I now know as yet another very common reaction from those who have been raped, especially those who have also been harmed sexually as children:

"I don't know if you would call it that. I always think I could have done more to fight him off."

She was blaming herself. The distortion of this protective reality is maddening and also very understandable. Better to think we have some power than comprehend we are purely a victim. Again, with the anger of injustice, I asked,

"Did you tell your mother?"

I am not sure why, but it was so easy for me to focus the blame on the one who didn't keep her safe, rather than her selfish great-uncle who should have known better or the man from the boarding house who took advantage knowing he would likely never be held to account.

How much easier it is to turn your wrath on the non-offending mother. Even with no information I quickly cast judgment. I have watched so many people do this in my life. A desperate attempt to find blame with someone other than the person responsible, rather than take in that we are somewhat powerless to protect our children from this kind of harm. I had known my great-grandmother Frida personally, and while she was long gone from this world at the time of this conversation, I was re-writing who she was to me with every word.

"I did tell her. She slapped my face and blamed me for seducing him. She let him continue to live in the boarding house. He would come into my room at night whenever he wanted. I would try to push the dresser in front of the door so he couldn't get in. Some nights I would beg her to let me sleep on her bedroom floor. As I say this now, I am not sure I ever got over her not protecting me. When I think back to those weeks she was dying, I was still holding it against her."

Here, for the first time, I saw the pain on her face. Was it pain from not being protected, feeling the vulnerability of her child self as she spoke or maybe from not having forgiven her mother before she died? I don't know. I didn't think to ask. As far as I knew, my grandmother had been a devoted daughter caring for Frida in her old age, up through her death. Listening to her confess she had closed her heart to a mother I know she had loved deeply is one of the long lasting tragedies of child sexual abuse. At 95 years old she was still feeling that pain.

She was gone now, lost in some memory as she looked out the window. "Oh, Mama," I heard her whisper, regret and anger meshing together.

I wish I had softened my own anger as she reached out in spirit to Frida. She was processing her conflict and confronting her feelings even at this late stage of her life. As I think about that now, it is truly incredible that 80-90 years later, she would start to reorganize her trauma, and come to see the long lasting impact it had on her life and relationships. The human spirit never ceases to amaze me.

At the time, I kept on my detective hat, looking for a deeper understanding of these past generations of people who lived whole lives before I came along. As in most families, we have the folklore passed down through stories. The immigrant struggle, the alcoholism, The Great Depression and the harsh winters. The historical events that shaped our ancestors' lives. This particular part of our folklore was new to me. While I was thinking about what else I wanted to know, my grandmother reached for a more stable place in her heart to hold the memory of her mother.

"Well, she didn't have it easy either. When she was a young girl, her father had a terrible drinking problem. She would be sent away to live on an uncle's farm, far from her own mother, whenever he fell off the wagon. She hated it there. She missed her own mother so much. She used to cry every time she thought about it. Right up until her deathbed, she was talking about hating being sent to his farm."

"Is that the same uncle that used to pay you a nickel?" I wondered out loud, knowing full well what the answer would be.

My grandmother looked up at me suddenly, the light bulb going off and said, "Yes. Yes it was."

My memory ends there. I don't recall how the conversation concluded though one of us likely changed the subject to escape from this topic. I do not know who was more relieved to move on from it, her or me. I do know, in this very brief but poignant interaction, she opened a door to healing, to understanding the distortions of our family folklore and perhaps, I hope, dissipated a small part of the intergenerational shame we carry collectively.

I regret not having said with deep compassion, "Thank you for telling me that painful story. I am so sorry you went through that when you were so young. I imagine it has impacted you in so many ways. I love you, and will be here for you in any way you need, whenever you want to process this with me."

Looking back it seems like it would have been so easy to say that, but I know it was not. I have grown a lot in the twenty-five years since that conversation. I see how I was overwhelmed with emotion, and not able to see the many layers of a disclosure such as this. She did what so many victims do.

She denied her reality until she could speak it. Her mother blamed her and so she internalized a culpability that wasn't hers, and then spent a lifetime minimizing what happened to her.

I never brought up the topic again to her, nor she to me. I imagine she spent her remaining years holding all of that alone. As she had done for 90 years, she set it aside and lived her life as best she could. After that day, life went back to the way it was.

I lost my grandmother three years later. I try to assign the distance I felt in our relationship in those final years to her age, to living halfway across the country, to having started my own family. I do feel that I let her down that day. I let myself down too. The chance to support someone more fully and consciously through their healing was missed.

It wasn't until my forties, that I began the hard work of addressing my own child sexual abuse history, and the sexual trauma I endured as a teenager. I now understand why it might have taken my grandmother so many decades to disclose the harm she endured as a child and young person. It takes a long time, and great strength, to start the work of facing the ways this kind of betrayal can impact a whole life.

I didn't tell anyone I was abused, not even myself. I endured child molestation, sexual attacks, date rape, and various forms of sexual harassment, as many others have. I lived dangerously, and put myself in harm's way many times. I struggled with addiction, moved and moved again, and avoided connection. I broke up with the good guys, and stayed with the ones who hurt me. These symptoms of abuse are not unique to me.

I eventually hit an emotional wall and got into therapy. My therapist and I didn't work on sexual abuse, because I still hadn't fully recalled those memories. Instead, she and I worked on getting sober, moving out of a dangerous neighborhood, changing my friends and associates, building the skills I needed to have healthy, appropriate boundaries with others, and learning about my own self-care.

It was a lot of work to undo the ways I had learned to cope with my past trauma, and then start to face the consequences of my own behavior. Addressing the sexual harm as a child and teenager was something else. It was buried beneath the trauma reactions that grew out of it. I needed to start on the surface before I was ready to face the harm underneath in a meaningful way.

The fog of my own abuse started to lift when I saw this pattern repeating itself in the next generation of my family. As sobriety, stability and frankly more maturity started to bring a groundedness to my life, I started to have the strength to face what I had been through. I finally understood that I am a victim, caught in a torrent of inherited sexual harm, stretching back to my great-grandmother and likely even further.

Five generations of child sexual abuse were coming into focus for me. I felt rageful, not for myself but for others. The anger replaced the shame and I began talking about my sexual harm with others. The secrecy and the tendency to brush this kind of thing under the rug suddenly seemed entirely unacceptable. I started to talk about it, and somehow talking about it freed me more. I told myself, 'Not another child in this family. This must stop. I am going to stop this from happening again'.

I founded Hidden Water in my mid forties, a non-profit dedicated to helping families heal from child sexual abuse, and stop abuse from reaching the next generation. Through that work, I learned the only way to help others is to face the impact the trauma has had on oneself. I couldn't have done my grandmother's work for her. I could only have loved and supported her as she did her own work. In order to be able to do that better, though, I would have had to do my own healing.

Regardless of when we are ready to start the work of healing, it can be done. Healing is not easy, but the journey is not without hope. It begins with just one person saying "enough!" and then taking the first steps to speak it out loud. Any individual, regardless of their relationship to the abuse, can start down this path.

The journey outlined in this book unfolded for me in unexpected ways. I have grown immensely from being the person in my family to say 'enough'. I discovered a path to my own healing that I hadn't fully realized I needed. In doing so, I inadvertently supported many others on their healing journeys. Indeed, it is often through hardship that we expand our community and evolve spiritually.

Healing from sexual harm, as a child, young person or as an adult, is nurtured by two seeds. The first is the brave act of sharing one's traumatic experience with another. It often takes years for survivors to reach a point where they are ready to disclose the abuse they have endured. When they are ready, and take the chance to share even in a small way, that is a sacred moment.

The second seed is planted when someone witnesses this disclosure with compassion. As trusted listeners, we contribute deeply to the healing process by creating a loving, supportive space for the one sharing their story. Healing thrives in this exchange between the one revealing their pain and those who hold steady in the belief that together, we can overcome anything.

My grandmother planted the first seed when she shared her story with me. While I wasn't able to fully nurture that seed at the time, this book is my attempt to show others how to cultivate that second, vital seed of compassionate listening. It's part of my amends to her, and a guide for future generations. For those who still have the opportunity to go back and support a loved one's disclosure, and for those who may become that 'trusted other' in the future, let this book be your roadmap.

When it is time to heal, we can only heal together.

CHAPTER 2

Beyond the Binary

Our society seems profoundly powerless to prevent child sexual abuse. We are ill-equipped to respond appropriately to it, and grossly under-skilled at managing its impact. So it is perhaps as painful as it is predictable that sexual harm to children has been a large part of human history for countless generations.

The reality of child sexual abuse is both pervasive and deeply troubling: Imagine a classroom of 30 students. Statistically, 6 of those children will experience sexual abuse before reaching adulthood. This isn't just a number – it's the lived experience of millions of young people around the world.

Child sexual abuse knows no boundaries. It crosses all socio-economic, racial, religious, ethnic, and cultural lines. People of all gender identities are both harmed, and cause harm. According to the World Health Organization, globally, 1 in 5 women and 1 in 13 men report experiencing sexual abuse before turning 18 years old. The true scope of this issue is even more startling.

Youth are 2.3 times more likely to experience sexual assault than adults.

In the U.S. alone, over 42 million adults are survivors of childhood sexual abuse. Nearly half of them were abused by a family member.

Perhaps most heartbreaking is the cycle of harm: girls whose mothers experienced sexual abuse are 3.6 times more likely to be abused themselves. Imagine that as an opportunity for prevention that goes tragically unrealized. These numbers represent real lives, real pain, and an urgent need for change. This public health epidemic is preventable.

Child sexual abuse often feels like a distant problem, something that happens to "other people." But the reality is much closer to home, literally. The greatest vulnerability for children often lies within their own homes and trusted circles of relationships.

- **88% of child sexual abuse goes unreported to authorities.**
- **82.9% of victims do not report rape they experience in childhood.**
- **It is estimated that more than 55% of adults have never shared their abuse in childhood with anyone.**
- **Half of those who did not disclose as children did not recognize it as abuse until adulthood.**

While these facts and figures illustrate the enormity of sexual abuse, this book won't be driven by statistics. Instead, we'll focus on human experiences and practical approaches to healing, repair and prevention.

By sharing these statistics, I hope to shine a light on a shared experience that too many have felt they had to face alone. If you or your family has been impacted by child sexual abuse, know this: You are part of a vast, often invisible community of survivors and families. Your experience, while deeply personal, is unfortunately far from uncommon.

This is not about normalizing abuse, but it is very much about normalizing the conversation around it. By recognizing how widespread this issue is, and talking about it, we can break down the isolation that so often accompanies individuals and families. As much as these statistics are startling (because they are), they also carry an important message:

If your family has been impacted by child sexual abuse, you are not alone. There is hope for healing, for change, and for breaking the cycle of silence and abuse.

Getting a fuller picture of child sexual abuse—its prevalence, the various attributes of those who are at risk of harming, common settings where harm happens, and the rarity of disclosure—is foundational. Knowledge alone is not enough, however. We must hone our ability to recognize and intervene when boundaries are crossed, preventing escalation to more severe forms of abuse.

We must also learn to respond appropriately to a child's disclosure, whether it's a clear statement or a tentative "half disclosure" stemming from their limited vocabulary or understanding. The journey to becoming a safe adult who can manage a disclosure with discernment and action without becoming overwhelmed themselves takes education, practice and support.

By opening our eyes to the fact that all actions have both intended and unintended consequences, we equip ourselves to better protect children and support survivors. By moving beyond simple solutions to an active awareness of the role we will play, and how it can be expanded in any situation, we will grow into safe(r) adults.

I was 19 when I took a job as a counselor at a summer camp nestled on a lake in my home state of Minnesota. The camp director, a man whose manner we initially dismissed as eccentricities, soon became a source of unease among the staff. His nightly visits to the younger boys' cabins, ostensibly to check for "ticks," raised eyebrows, but we couldn't quite articulate why it felt so wrong.

A couple weeks into the season, the director pulled a ten-year-old boy onto his lap, pretending to tickle him, and grabbed his testicles. The boy immediately jumped up and ran to his counselors, but said nothing. Later that evening, this camper was hanging out with some of us by the campfire. One of the adult counselors was talking comically about how the director was always walking into the men's showers to chat and we were all laughing.

The boy, feeling safe to join in, told us what had happened to him with the director. In hindsight, I can see now he was hoping we would lump it in with the rest of the stories, and laugh. He found some normalizing explanation for his experience: the "strangeness" of this director was what other people were dealing with too. I sometimes imagine if we had just laughed with him, this event might have faded for him. Instead, we all went silent, looking at each other with wide eyes.

The next day, after one of us called our mom, who then called Child Protective Services, we waited to see what would happen. We said nothing to the boy because we knew nothing, and didn't have the maturity to know how to act. We were all probably thinking we didn't want to be confronted by our boss. Within 24 hours, child protective services came and removed the director from the camp. Soon after, the boy was picked up by his parents and brought home.

The director was arrested and released on bail, but we did not see him again for the rest of the summer. In fact, I never saw him again.

My heart ached for the young camper as I imagined

him recounting his story over and over to a parade of well-meaning but often insensitive adults. His parents, their anger and protectiveness palpable, struggled to navigate a system that seemed designed to re-traumatize rather than help. The doubt expressed by prosecutors about securing a conviction I can only imagine felt like a betrayal, leaving the family feeling as if they had somehow failed their son.

The trial was a cruel farce. The camp director's attorney insisted the boy made it up for attention. Surely, he claimed, the boy misunderstood the director's intentions and affection. In the end, the director was found not guilty for lack of evidence.

This incident represents one of the rare cases where child sexual abuse was reported to law enforcement and resulted in a criminal trial. In this challenging situation, those responsible for the boy's safety – teenage counselors, parents, and camp administrators – relied on state mechanisms, as these were the only resources anyone knew about.

In the full timeline of responding to the disclosure, each decision point presented a catch-22, beginning with my fellow counselors and me. We could have chosen not to report it, potentially protecting this child for the remainder of the summer on our own. However, this decision would likely have allowed the director to continue harming others. Reporting it, though necessary, set in motion a series of events that undoubtedly compounded the boy's trauma.

To their credit, the parents' first act was to believe their son, though I'll note that this is likely easier when the offender is an outsider to the family. They took him home, cooperated with the investigation, and brought charges against the director. While seeking criminal justice may seem like the natural and appropriate response to most, the results are not so straightforward.

At a time when this boy needed guidance on how to understand this molestation, the community response inadvertently intensified his pain. He was abruptly removed from camp mid-summer, in full view of friends and counselors, with rumors swirling. I remember how the feelings of shame started immediately with our collective silence after his disclosure. I imagine he was internalizing his parents' distress, possibly even wishing he had never spoken up.

I stand by the decision to call Child Protective Services. It was better for the community that we spoke out, eventually leading to the director's removal from the camp. This was undoubtedly humiliating for the boy. I am unsure if anyone reassured him that it wasn't his fault. Society often blames victims in the harshest ways.

As far as I know, the director never returned to the camp. However, I did hear he later married a struggling single mother with young boys. Over the years, I would hear about his "troubled stepchildren," each of whom had attempted to run away multiple times. While we may have protected one group of children, as a community, we failed to bring about a true solution.

Our society's primary responses to child sexual abuse—immediate safety interventions and the criminal justice system—are often insufficient or even harmful. While ensuring a child's safety is critical, these systems frequently fail to consider the full complexity of the family system, leaving many cases unreported and families hesitant to seek help. The criminal justice system, in particular, is a blunt instrument that prioritizes legal action over a nuanced approach to healing and long-term safety.

Families fear that involving child protective services will lead to rigid, sometimes arbitrary oversight, known as family policing, which can impose requirements that do little to address the root causes of harm. This system, often criticized for its racial disparities and bureaucratic inefficiencies, focuses on compliance rather than genuine support, leaving families feeling scrutinized rather than helped.

Yet the alternative—managing alone in silence—is just as inadequate. A third path exists: one that prioritizes survivor-centered, family-led responses while integrating outside support as needed. This approach does not dismiss the role of law enforcement or protective intervention when there is an immediate risk to a child's safety. Instead, it recognizes that in many cases, families can be supported to take an active role in ensuring safety, accountability, and healing. Every family has the potential for strong, safe adult leadership—adults who, when given the right tools and guidance, can create protective environments that reflect their unique strengths and needs.

Despite the vast resources allocated to criminal justice—incarceration, offender registries, child protective services, foster care, and mental health services for survivors—the most effective form of prevention remains largely overlooked: family-based prevention. Few political efforts focus on stopping intergenerational harm before it begins, even though prevention would reduce the long-term social and economic costs of abuse.

To truly address child sexual abuse, we must move beyond conventional solutions. Families are not just sites of harm; they are also human systems with the only potential for healing. With the right support, they can become the strongest force in preventing and addressing abuse. By shifting our focus toward empowering safe adults within families—while ensuring that external interventions are used thoughtfully and appropriately—we can create lasting change, break cycles of harm, and foster a future where families are equipped to protect and heal their own.

CHAPTER 3

Betrayal After the Harm

Healing from sexual abuse is not a linear process. Sometimes, we are confronted with situations that bring old wounds to the surface. Resilience is tested and exposing the deep-seated impact of not just the initial harm, but also the responses of those we count on. Family dynamics can compound the trauma of sexual abuse, creating layers of betrayal that persist long after the original incident.

A Green Story: *Betrayal Trauma*

Sharah's excitement was palpable as she approached her childhood home, the soft silk of her new South Indian sari swishing gently against her skin. The prospect of a pleasant evening hosting her parents' dinner party had filled her with warmth and anticipation. As she stepped through the front door, looking around with a bright open smile on her face, the sound of laughter and cheerful chatter abruptly turned into a dull roar in her ears. There, at the head of the table, sat the religious leader who had sexually abused her as a young teen. His sly knowing look, directed right at her, froze her in place.

The confusion broke when her mother rushed over, thrusting a tray of food into her hands and gesturing towards her abuser. Sharah looked at her mother in silent disbelief, her mind racing to comprehend the surreal scene unfolding before her. In that moment, the part of her that recognized the wrongness of this situation retreated, leaving her feeling hollow and disconnected. Her emotions, lost somewhere, were going to have to wait. She would search and find them later.

As Sharah stood there, rooted to the spot, memories flooded back unbidden. She remembered the months of manipulation, the way he had twisted her naive devotion into a sexual relationship, her first. She had believed herself special, loved, even if it had to remain a secret. The cruel awakening came when he moved on to the next younger girl, revealing the true nature of what she had been to him.

Adult Sharah now understood it for what it was: the sexual exploitation of a minor. The weight of her parents' reaction when she had finally told them years ago pressed down on her. Their grief and fear had been palpable, but so too had been their insistence on silence. "Don't speak of it again," they had pleaded. "He's respected in the community. No one would believe you. We'd be shunned." Their words had sentenced her to decades of silent suffering, struggling through college and adulthood while presenting a facade of normalcy to her beloved parents who relied on her more and more as they aged.

Now, standing in her childhood home with a tray of food meant for her abuser, Sharah felt as though she were underwater. Sounds became muffled, movements slowed, and the edges of her vision blurred. Her mother's nervous nudge barely registered as she watched him from across the room, his obliviousness to the distress he was causing.

On legs that felt disconnected from her body, Sharah moved forward. Each step towards her abuser felt like a betrayal of her younger self, of the years of healing she had fought so hard for. As she offered him the food, his smile widened, and the knowing look in his eyes made her skin crawl. In that silent exchange, Sharah realized he viewed their past as a shared secret, a consensual relationship. The rage rising in her throat.

With herculean effort, Sharah managed a stiff, polite smile in return. She navigated the rest of the evening on autopilot, falling back into the well-worn patterns of putting her parents' needs before her own. It was a familiar dance, one she had performed countless times over the years, but never had it felt so devastating.

In the weeks that followed, Sharah sank into a deep depression. The encounter had ripped open old wounds, pouring salt into injuries she thought had long since healed. As she slowly began to emerge from a fog of despair, a question haunted her: "Why am I not over this yet?"

Sharah knew the answer, though, she just needed to let it come to the surface. This wasn't just about the abuse she had suffered as a teen. It was about the ongoing betrayal by those who should have protected her. The silencing of her pain for the sake of social propriety. The expectation that she should simply "get over" a trauma that had shaped her entire life.

Later, sitting alone in her apartment, far from her childhood home, she realized true healing couldn't come from burying the past or pretending it didn't affect her. It would only come from acknowledging the full scope of her experience. Not just the initial abuse, but the years of enforced silence and the recent betrayal of her parents. It would come from setting boundaries, from prioritizing her own well-being over familial expectations, and from giving herself permission to feel anger, grief, and everything in between.

The road ahead would be challenging. It would mean confronting her parents, risking relationships, and possibly facing disbelief or rejection from her community. Sharah took a deep breath, she felt a spark of determination ignite within her. She had survived the abuse, she had survived the silence, and she would survive this too. More than that, she would thrive, reclaiming her voice and her power, one courageous step at a time.

Recognizing that the harm had just been inflicted anew was a significant shift in perspective for Sharah. When our loved ones minimize or ignore our lived experiences, the harm doesn't end—it continues, perpetuated in a very real way. In Sharah's case, this came from her parents. The failure to protect us when we are young and vulnerable is the inherent betrayal of child sexual abuse. When our loved ones, even in adulthood, fail to protect us emotionally, it can reopen that wound, making us feel the harm all over again.

Sharah's parents, likely believing the harm was firmly in the past, failed to recognize the lasting impact of their own actions. They assumed their daughter had moved on from that episode in her life long ago.

When asked by the community to host the religious leader, they saw it as an honor not easily declined. Probably they didn't anticipate the devastating impact it would have on their daughter to be suddenly in the presence of her offender.

The belief that time heals all wounds can be especially damaging in cases of child sexual abuse. Survivors often internalize this idea, assuming that something from the distant past should no longer affect them. But time alone does not heal these wounds. If anything, it can sharpen awareness of their lasting consequences. Pain does not simply fade; it resurfaces again and again, especially when a survivor experiences betrayal or even a perceived betrayal. With a heightened sense that people cannot be trusted, survivors often struggle to rebuild relationships.

Trust is fragile in the aftermath of sexual harm. It can be further eroded when family members fail to consider a survivor's needs, whether by minimizing the impact, avoiding difficult conversations, or assuming that moving on is the same as healing. When child sexual abuse is only partially addressed, as in cases where it is discussed once and never spoken of again, the survivor is often left to carry the weight alone while others move on, unaware of the lasting effects. Pain that is suppressed does not disappear. Instead, it shifts, intensifies, and creates emotional barriers that can strain relationships for years.

Families who do not fully acknowledge or work through the harm risk allowing trauma to fester, fueling cycles of conflict and disconnection. Healing is not a single conversation or a box to be checked. It requires attention over time, creating space for the aftermath to gradually fade and the impact to lessen. The effects of trauma may lie dormant for years, only to resurface in moments of stress, change, or new betrayals.

To truly move forward, families must find ways to work through the aftermath together. This does not require absolute agreement on every detail, but it does require a shared vocabulary and an agreed upon basic understanding that what happened was harmful. Without this, meaningful conversations remain out of reach, and disconnection continues. Families that commit to engaging with the truth create the conditions for repair, making healing possible for both the survivor and the family as a whole.

A Green Story: *Betrayal Trauma*

Tara stared at her phone in disbelief. Her father's group text message to the family chat burned her eyes. The image of her grandfather, smiling openly at the camera as he held up a fish while embracing his grandchildren in a boat. The caption read: "Happy Birthday, Dad! We miss you!" All the heart emojis showing up to celebrate the text, and honor the man on his birthday, who had been gone for many years.

At that moment, she lost her appetite. She felt tired and crawled into her bed. The grandfather so fondly remembered by her father was the same man who had stolen her innocence, who had violated her trust in the most horrific way during her grade school years.

Tears blurred Tara's vision as she lay in bed alone. This seemingly innocuous, even heartwarming message from her father was a wrecking ball to her emotional stability. Tara had invested years in therapy, support groups, and self-help techniques, gradually reclaiming her life from the shadow of abuse. She was thriving in many ways, but now that wound had reopened.

The persistent ache, the thorn that refused to be dislodged, was her family's unwavering veneration of the man who abused her. They had known about the abuse since Tara's twenties, yet they continued to elevate her grandfather as the beloved man who was always wonderful (to them). He retained the high regard everyone had always had of him, in his last years of life, and in death.

When Tara's dad was told about the abuse, he went to see his father and asked him about it directly. His father did not have the reaction he was expecting. He thought he would be shocked, and concerned for Tara. Instead, he looked guilty, and got up with a sigh to pour himself some coffee. He eventually offered to his son "I don't really remember doing anything all that bad to her. I certainly didn't mean to upset her."

Tara's father was shocked and left immediately without another word. He fell into a depression and very little attention was paid to Tara about what she was going through. Her siblings were told by their mother but beyond a few 'we are so sorry that happened to you' no one said much else.

There was disappointment and grief in the family for months but it faded with time. Then, they started talking about him again, and mentioning that they had seen him. Before long, the grandfather was showing up to family gatherings without anyone registering how that might be for Tara to see him now that the family was aware of what happened.

He died a few years later, and that was a relief for Tara. Now, she would not have to navigate her hurt feelings and the disconnection she felt to her family members. It was relatively calm for a while but somehow this text message hit her in the wrong way, at the wrong time.

The bitterness and resentment that Tara had worked so hard to overcome these past many years since her grandfather's death came rushing back with a vengeance. With shaking hands, Tara forwarded the text to me. Her message read: "Can you believe this shit? I need a break from these people. I am not going home for a LONG time. I need to start prioritizing myself, once I am able to get out of my bed."

The effects of past abuse can show up in various family situations, from major life events to the smallest everyday interactions. These moments can strain the fragile equilibrium families try to maintain to prevent reopening old wounds. In their efforts to avoid conflict, family members tip toe around the subject creating an atmosphere of unspoken tension and suppressed emotions.

Healing begins when we acknowledge the unique dynamics abuse has created within our family system. Identifying what exacerbates the situation for each family member can be a formidable catalyst for positive change. If Tara's family chooses to understand how their actions or inactions are fracturing their relationship with her, and instead courageously confront their discomfort with her pain, they could gradually rebuild trust.

Expecting the one who was harmed to heal entirely on their own while we resume normal family life is not fair or effective. It transfers all the responsibility onto the survivor to bear the weight. If everyone was to take part in that process, the work of healing can be distributed more evenly, lightening everyone's load. After all, shouldn't everyone feel betrayed by the harm caused by the grandfather, and curious about why, how and from where this behavior came?

Family members must get braver. They can't wait for the survivor to lead the conversation. There is enough burden on the one who was harmed sexually. Someone else in the family can take charge of how the grandfather's birthday can be acknowledged without losing sight of the damage he had done.

It's possible to honor family members who have caused harm for the complex individuals they are, but this must include a genuine acknowledgment of the harm and an awareness of the ongoing impact those who were affected will potentially always be suffering from. We're not trying to paint over the reality to make it look the way we wish it had been. Nor do we soften the impact by focusing on someone's strengths or other positive traits. We face the situation as it is, in all its messiness, and begin from there.

Small, thoughtful actions can make a significant difference. If Tara's mother checked in after the text, if a sibling privately discussed being more sensitive with their father, or if her father recognized what he had done thoughtlessly even if not intentionally and apologized, Tara might feel more inclined to reconnect.

Healing a family system requires noticing and taking responsibility for unintentional missteps, owning past failures, and demonstrating a strong willingness to repair relationships. There are no shortcuts, but a family made more resilient through meaningful and lasting repair is worth the effort.

CHAPTER 4

Our Part To Play

When sexual abuse occurs within a family, the choice to remain still or step up shapes the course of everyone's lives. We can stand by, passive, disconnected or silent, or we can engage with courage and intention. Either way our actions—or inactions—reverberate throughout the family. Our decision carries weight, influencing not only the well-being of those directly harmed but also the integrity and future of the family as a whole.

We can choose to be bystanders, watching from the sidelines, or upstanders, actively engaging as a full member of the system. An upstander is someone who speaks out or takes action to support others, becoming a force for positive change. Popularized in anti-bullying efforts, this concept challenges us to move beyond passively witnessing pain or harm and to embrace the responsibility of making a difference in whatever way we can.

It is unrealistic to expect those who have been harmed to navigate their healing journey alone while others merely await their recovery. This approach breeds resentment, leads to estrangement, and perpetuates dysfunction. The survivor should not bear the responsibility of instructing others on how to do their own work to heal. As adults, we must proactively determine our role in fostering healing.

Every family member is affected by the harm, whether they became aware of it early on or joined the family later. Without conscious effort to play a supportive role, we risk unintentionally reinforcing harmful dynamics or hindering progress. Being a silent bystander is far from neutral. In fact, it can be the opposite. Inaction aligns us with not recovering, and often makes the situation worse.

When family members step up as upstanders, they create momentum for change. Educating ourselves, speaking up when something feels wrong, and reinforcing safe boundaries can spark meaningful shifts within the family system. At first, engaging in these conversations may feel uncomfortable or even create conflict. However, when we approach them with compassion, ask thoughtful questions, and challenge harmful patterns with care, we open the door to transformation. This is not about addressing a single moment of harm; it is about fostering lasting, positive change within the family.

Navigating healing after sexual harm requires ongoing effort and intentional action. Three key skills help lay the foundation for healthier family dynamics: engaging in internal work, establishing healthy boundaries, and holding space for others. These practices allow us to rebuild trust, strengthen connections, and create an environment where healing is possible.

The Internal Work

Internal work is the cornerstone of family healing. It is a constructive self absorption. We are attending to ourselves. It involves a deep, introspective journey of self-discovery and self-care. By examining our own past, our own lived experiences and understanding how they've shaped who we are, we can initiate meaningful emotional and behavioral shifts.

This is not an exploration of how the victim was impacted. This isn't even about our feelings for them. This is building an understanding of how the harm has impacted us individually. Where is our anger, our guilt, our devastation? How do we feel betrayed by others or the circumstances? What if we were to give voice to our own resentment? How does this relate to the unique position we hold in the family? What re-examination is required of our own relationships with others now?

Internal work is the ongoing commitment to understanding ourselves more deeply. It is essential to recognizing and overcoming harmful or self-defeating patterns. While this self-exploration does not absolve us of responsibility for the ways we may have negatively impacted others, it allows us to respond with greater awareness and act in ways that build connection rather than break it down.

Engaging in internal work is not about assigning blame. The more we understand the experiences that have shaped us—both big and small—the better we can see how they influence the dynamics we navigate today. With this awareness, we can cultivate greater compassion for ourselves and others. Compassion does not mean bypassing anger, excusing harm, or minimizing its effects. Instead, it is a deeper acknowledgment of each person's humanity, including our own, as we move through the difficult process of healing.

For each family member, this process begins with grounding themselves in a deep understanding of how the abuse has affected them personally. By recognizing and valuing our unique internal experiences of the harm—not just the sexual abuse but all related incidents—we can cultivate a renewed sense of stability, strength, and determination. This personal growth lays the foundation for stepping into the role of an upstander within our family system.

Internal work is the preliminary step before a family can begin healing together. It is the individual process of examining our own blind spots, biases, and emotional reactions without placing that burden on others in the family. This work should happen outside the family system so that each adult can take responsibility for their own growth without unintentionally causing further harm.

The one who was sexually harmed should not have to listen to family members as they struggle to make sense of their own misunderstandings or emotional discomfort. While self-exploration is necessary, it is unfair to expect the survivor to teach others why certain words or perspectives are hurtful.

Likewise, the person who caused the sexual harm (when they are a part of the family unit) must do their own internal work, separate from the emotions and processing of other family members. Expecting them to hold space for others before they have had a chance to process their own understanding of how they came to harm in this way can interfere with their ability to take accountability and engage in meaningful exchanges.

To do this work effectively, each person needs a source of support outside the family. This might include therapy, support groups, online communities, or trusted mentors who can offer a safe space to listen and offer guidance without judgment. Engaging in this process allows us to examine how our own past experiences shape our reactions and perspectives, so that when the time comes to work together as a family, we are better prepared to listen and contribute to real healing.

This increased self-awareness fosters compassion, first for ourselves and ultimately for others, which can positively transform our family interactions. Dedicating time to our inner work helps us define our role in supporting the family as a whole, including ourselves and each member of the system. It also provides clarity about what is not our responsibility, allowing us to set healthy boundaries and avoid fruitless attempts to rescue others or fix it for them.

Engaging in this internal work creates a foundation for better communication, deeper empathy, and meaningful healing within the family system. While it requires a commitment of time and potentially resources to seek the support needed, it is a necessary step toward becoming an active contributor to the family's healing process.

Setting Healthy Boundaries

Healthy boundaries are the limits we establish around our time, energy, physical body, and emotional state to maintain our resilience and live our lives as we see fit. These boundaries protect us from feeling overwhelmed, drained, or manipulated by others. They also help us recognize that each person is responsible for their own well-being as an adult, preventing us from carrying burdens that are not ours to hold.

As we deepen our self-understanding, we gain a greater appreciation for boundaries and recognize our role within the family, as well as those roles that do not belong to us. Healthy boundaries create a safer environment for everyone to coexist.

It begins with acknowledging that each adult is responsible for their own healing journey – they alone direct it and are accountable for it. A corollary to this is that each person has autonomy in their own healing journey. This includes independence in deciding whether or not to embark on that journey.

Blaming, criticizing, or demanding that others change may be understandable, but it is ultimately counterproductive. The more we try to control others, the more resistance we create. We exhaust ourselves trying to make people behave as we wish they would, but true change can only come from within. Letting go of this struggle allows us to reclaim our energy for something far more productive—our own healing.

Accepting others as they are, at least for now, frees us from seeking our healing outside of ourselves. This does not mean we excuse harmful behavior or surrender to unhealthy dynamics. It means we stop suffering over what we wish were true and start working with what is actually true. The reality of who someone is today may not be who they will always be, but they must come to their own understanding on their own timeline. When we stop trying to force change, we create the space for genuine transformation to take root.

As we stop trying to manage others' reactions, actions, or inactions, we give them the freedom to find their own meaningful path. If someone only changes because we pressured them to, their words and actions will always feel hollow and uncertain. Change that is self-motivated is the only change that holds real weight.

Stepping back also allows the family system to shift in response to individual growth. Families develop deeply ingrained patterns, and even small disruptions to these patterns can unsettle others causing a sense that the person setting healthy boundaries is being cruel.

It is common to feel guilty when the people we love struggle with the changes we are making. But compromising our own integrity to ease their discomfort only leads to resentment. Real change is uncomfortable, but that discomfort is part of the process. If we stand firm in our boundaries while remaining kind and patient, the family has a chance to adjust over time in ways that are ultimately healthier for everyone.

Letting go of unrealistic expectations of others does not mean giving up on what we need. It means redirecting our energy toward affirming our right to safety, dignity, and self-care. Instead of trying to make others meet our needs, we focus on establishing boundaries that honor our well-being.

Boundaries are not about controlling others; they are about taking responsibility for ourselves. This means respecting others' autonomy as well. We do not demand that others change for us, just as we do not allow them to override our own agency. When each person is responsible for themselves, healthier dynamics begin to emerge.

Healing within a family requires a shared reality, but that reality cannot be forced or dictated by one person. If we dominate the family narrative, pushing only our perspective, we create resistance rather than understanding. Our perspective may be the least distorted one, but insisting on it only causes others to resist. We can live from our reality, absolutely. And, healing together is a collaborative process, not something that can be imposed.

Instead of trying to control how others see things, we cultivate curiosity about their experiences while maintaining our own boundaries. We listen, we share, and we watch what unfolds. The goal is not to achieve a perfect agreement but to co-create a dynamic where everyone feels 'safe enough' and participates voluntarily. When one person dictates the terms, the foundation remains unstable. When each person engages from their own authentic place, honors the boundaries set by others, the family has the potential to evolve in ways we never could have predicted.

The Art of Holding Space

Holding space means being fully present with another person's inner world—witnessing their perspective, experiences, and emotions without imposing our own or passing judgment. It requires offering undivided attention and creating an environment where others feel safe to express their truth without fear of correction or interference. Unlike typical conversations, where ideas are exchanged and debated, holding space prioritizes listening over responding. The listener remains attentive and receptive, allowing the speaker to fully express themselves without interruption, unsolicited advice, or competing opinions.

This practice is especially valuable when someone is overwhelmed by emotions and needs a safe, non-judgmental space to process their feelings. When we listen with curiosity—simply seeking to understand rather than evaluate—we offer something rare and powerful. Something shifts when we feel truly heard. Holding space requires an intentional internal alignment, where the listener consciously sets aside their own reactions, beliefs, and assumptions. The goal is not to analyze, problem-solve, or provide a different perspective but to allow the speaker's reality to exist as it is in that moment.

It helps to remember that what someone expresses is a snapshot of their inner world at a particular time, not a permanent truth. By accepting what they share without jumping to conclusions about what it means in the long run, we create a subtle openness—one that, paradoxically, allows perspectives to evolve. When people feel the need to defend themselves, they become more entrenched in their position. But when they are met with acceptance, they naturally begin to explore beyond the limits of their current perspective.

Even when the speaker expresses intense or one-sided emotions, our role is to witness rather than correct. Pushing back against strong feelings often amplifies them, reinforcing frustration or resistance. In contrast, when we allow those emotions to be voiced without interference, they tend to lose their intensity and soften on their own. The speaker may not immediately adopt a broader perspective, but they will often experience a sense of relief, which creates space for deeper reflection and clarity to emerge organically.

Holding space also removes the burden from the speaker to manage our emotions, allowing for true self-expression. When we react with shock, overwhelm, or defensiveness, we unintentionally teach others that honesty comes at a cost. If sharing their feelings leads to us shutting down, arguing, or making it about our own pain, they will learn to withhold, edit, or soften their truth to avoid upsetting us. Over time, they will share less and less until the relationship becomes performative rather than authentic. Instead of a space for genuine connection, interactions become carefully managed to prevent conflict or discomfort.

This pattern often comes from fear, hurt, or our own unresolved pain, but the impact remains the same: we signal that we cannot hold space, and so we are entrusted with less. By listening without rushing to insert our own perspective, we build the kind of trust that invites others to keep turning toward us, rather than away. Slowly, the family culture shifts into one where inner experiences are not feared, dismissed, or managed but met with patience and understanding. When we learn to sit with what is, rather than reacting from a place of discomfort, we make room for natural healing to unfold in its own time.

The more we listen, the more we begin to truly know and understand the other person. We stop seeing them only through the lens of our own expectations and instead recognize how the world occurs to them. This shift deepens trust and strengthens our relationships, creating a sense of intimacy that would not be possible if we were focused on inserting our own worldview. By honoring their reality as they experience it, we build rapport rather than distance—giving us more access to that person, not less. Over time, as trust deepens, this approach can transform family dynamics, replacing fear and defensiveness with greater tolerance, patience, and compassion.

Internal work, healthy boundaries, and holding space for others' experiences are three intertwining threads that form a strong bond for healing together. As we cultivate these practices, we enhance our capacity to show up authentically and effectively for ourselves and those around us.

This story portrays a common disclosure scenario. While it doesn't yet show the application of internal work, boundaries, or holding space, it underscores why these elements are vital for the family's path toward restoration. This account lays the groundwork, revealing the raw emotions and layered dynamics that often arise before a deliberate effort to heal as a family begins.

A Green Story: *The line in the sand*

Jamie's entire body trembled, a physical manifestation of the emotional tsunami within him as he looked at his mother's face full of distress about what he might say. The words he had rehearsed countless times in his mind now seemed to stick in his throat. "I won't be attending Aunt Joan's funeral," he finally managed, his voice barely above a whisper.

His mother's reaction was swift and predictable. "Why?" she demanded, her tone shifting from confusion to indignation. "She is our family, Jamie! That is incredibly disrespectful. What will people think if you don't show up?"

The familiar weight of shame and obligation threatened to crush Jamie's resolve, but something had changed in him since his aunt's death. At 30, he was finally ready to speak his truth, no matter the cost. Taking a deep breath, he steeled himself and blurted out, "Mom, she... she molested me when I was young."

The words hung in the air between them, heavy and irrevocable. Jamie's voice quivered as he continued, unleashing years of pent-up pain and anger. He described in halting detail the years of abuse at the hands of his aunt, the woman his mother had just lost.

As he spoke, the intrusive memories played out in his mind's eye. The disgust reaction unsettled him. The years of silent suffering that had shaped his life in ways his family had never understood. It was time to let someone else hold this for a while, now that his aunt was gone.

His mother remained passive as Jamie poured out his heart, but he could see the storm brewing behind her eyes. When he finally fell silent, exhausted by his confession, she took a step back, physically distancing herself from his words.

"No," she said, her voice cold and flat. "Your aunt loved you like a son. You must be mistaken. I don't believe it. Why are you trying to ruin her now that she's not here to defend herself?"

Her denial hit Jamie with surprise. His carefully constructed courage crumbled in the face of his mother's disbelief. Mumbling something incoherent, he fled the house, the bitter taste of injustice and feeling unseen was more than he could bear.

Alone in his apartment, Jamie lay motionless, staring at the ceiling. Hours passed, marked only by the vibration of his phone as family members tried to reach him. His father's voice, his siblings' pleas were all variations on the same theme: "Think of your mother. She just lost her sister. Don't do this to her."

The irony wasn't lost on Jamie. In all their concern for his mother's grief, not a single person had paused to consider what he might be going through. The sudden death of the woman who had taken advantage of his vulnerability had unleashed a maelstrom of conflicting emotions: relief, anger, a sense of loss, and underneath it all, a simmering rage at the years of silence he had endured.

Fed up with the barrage of guilt-laden messages, Jamie finally turned off his phone. In the ensuing silence, he felt a curious mixture of emotions wash over him. Grief for the childhood he had lost, for the relationships forever altered by his aunt's actions, filled his chest like a physical ache. Yet alongside this familiar pain, he felt something new stirring for the first time.

In the darkness of his room, Jamie made a silent vow to himself. From this moment forward, he would no longer betray himself to mollify others' discomfort. The road ahead would be hard, fraught with difficult conversations and potentially irreparable rifts, but for the first time in years, Jamie felt a glimmer of hope. He had taken the first step on a long journey of healing, and there was no turning back now.

Jamie's disclosure was likely the result of deep personal work. His aunt's death may have reshaped his sense of safety and priorities, giving him the clarity and resolve to assert his boundaries. His decision not to attend the funeral was a defining moment—one that prioritized his well-being over family expectations. Far from selfish, this choice reflected a commitment to his healing and resilience.

For his mother, learning that her beloved sibling had harmed her child was undoubtedly shocking. Her initial denial, while painful for Jamie, was a common response to devastating information. With time and support, she can process the truth and do her own internal work to repair the relationship. His father, while struggling with the news himself, had an opportunity to model a more supportive response—one that acknowledged Jamie's pain and affirmed his autonomy, even while navigating his own emotions.

Jamie's family's pushback against his decision highlights how difficult it can be to respect boundaries when they challenge long-standing family norms. However, healthy relationships require honoring each other's choices, even when they are hard to accept. A more supportive response might have been:

"I'm so sorry, Jamie. Thank you for telling us. I can't fully process this right now, but we'll figure it out together. I support your decision about the funeral. Can we talk more next week when things have settled?"

Similarly, his mother's reaction, shaped by grief and disbelief, made it difficult for her to hold space for Jamie's disclosure. A more helpful response—one that allowed for future conversations—could have been:

"I... I don't know what to say. Thank you for telling me. I need time to process this. Can we talk more after the funeral?"

Healing from sexual harm within a family is a complex, ongoing process. It requires internal work, the setting of healthy boundaries, and the ability to hold space for each other's experiences. We will not always respond perfectly, but we can always return to repair. What matters most is how the family honors each member's self-determination and healing path as they evolve.

By practicing these skills, we transform difficult moments into opportunities for growth and connection. Missteps can be corrected with honesty and compassion. This work is challenging, but it is possible.

As Maya Angelou said, *"Do the best you can until you know better. Then when you know better, do better."*

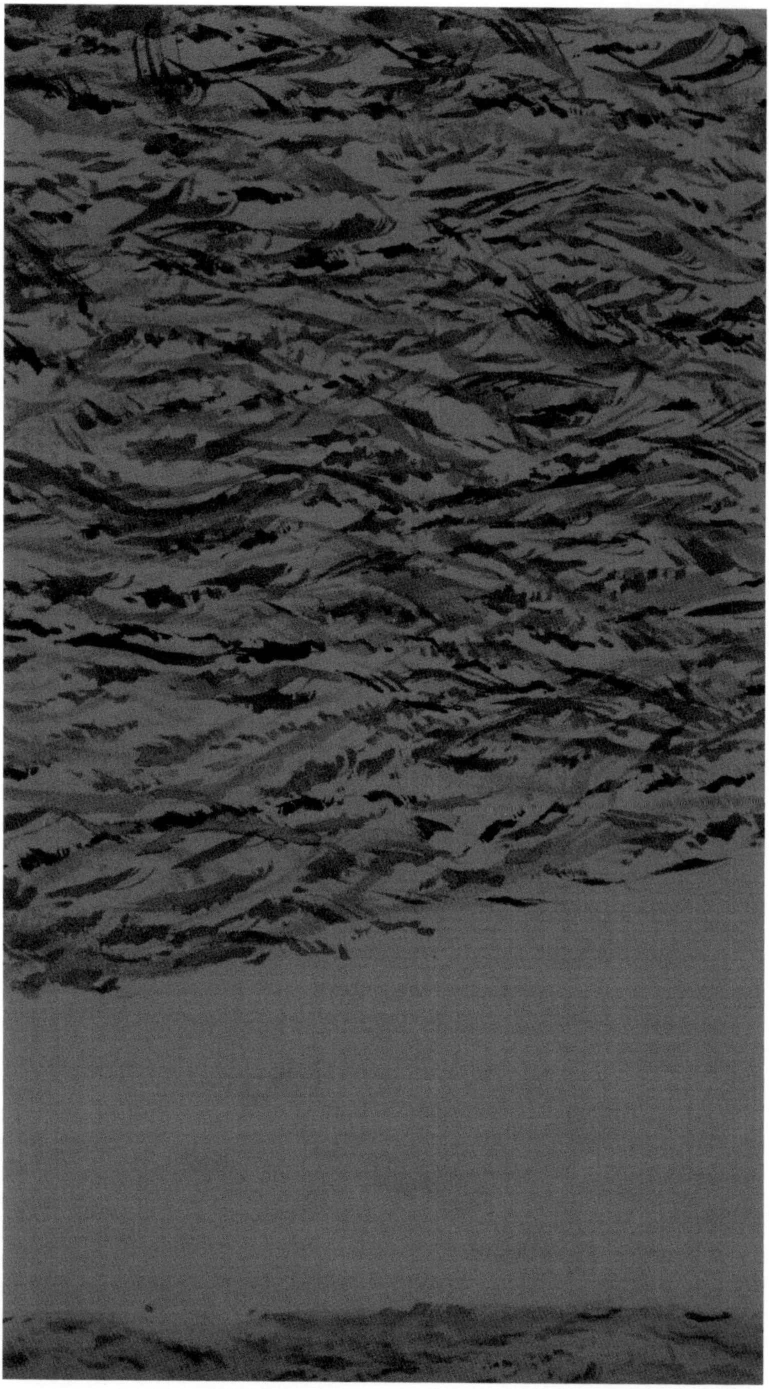

PART II

CHAPTER 5

Anatomy of Shame

The lasting impact of child sexual abuse can be difficult to comprehend. Understanding what makes that harm endure, often a lifetime, begins with examining shame. And to truly understand shame, we must first explore the concept of moral harm.

> *"To harm someone else morally is to communicate - through words or actions - that we think they are of less value or worth than ourselves and perhaps of no value at all. We have wronged someone when we send them the message that we see them as a mere object, rather than our equal. We regard them as little more than a means to our end. We see them as useful for our own purposes, regardless of what they want or how they might feel".*
>
> *Beyond Harm by Derek R. Brookes*

When I first read these words, I thought immediately of child sexual abuse. This definition, to me, communicates precisely why sexual harm has such a long lasting impact. While the physical act itself is undoubtedly harmful, it's in these words we find the root of the true damage inflicted. As a survivor of sexual harm, I find solace in the complexity of this definition. It provides language for an experience that often defies description.

Treating a young person as 'a mere object' or 'little more than a means to an end' captures the essence of this trauma in a way rarely articulated. When an adult who should protect a child instead exploits them for their own sexual gratification, disregarding their responsibility and instead takes advantage of this young person's vulnerability, it is a profound betrayal.

Sexual abuse disregards a child's inability to comprehend or navigate the complexity of a sexual relationship—especially with someone in a position of power. It is a violation that ignores the profound, long-term impact on the child, consequences that often extend far into adulthood.

This perspective helps us see why the effects of sexual abuse often persist long after the physical acts have ceased. It's not just about what happened to the body, but about the unspoken message communicated to the child's developing sense of self-worth and their place in the world. Understanding this can be an important step forward in the healing process, both for survivors, the one who caused the harm and for those supporting them.

Moral Harm and Injury

Child sexual abuse inflicts a 'moral injury', a concept that brings to light why its impact reverberates throughout a person's life. This harm can be elusive, manifesting in a myriad of symptoms that evolve over time, often obscuring its true nature. Its effects alter the life of not just the survivor but the entire social system surrounding them, sometimes in perplexing ways.

Moral harm strikes at the core of our basic dignity. Through words, actions, or even inactions, it communicates that we are 'of lesser value' than others and can be treated accordingly. When this message seeps into family dynamics—often unconsciously—it creates fractures that weaken the entire system. The result is often generations of discord, dysfunction, and a diminished capacity to thrive.

To better understand moral harm, it's important to distinguish it from other forms of trauma. Consider the survivors in a community devastated by a landslide. While they face deep trauma from the loss of life, home, and community, they are spared the additional burden of moral harm because nature's indifference does not communicate a message of worthlessness.

Now imagine the landslide was not a natural disaster but caused by a large mall constructed uphill, with developers knowingly diverting water in ways that created hazardous conditions for the community below. If the developers proceeded with construction despite knowing the risks, we see a clear example of moral harm. This willful disregard for others' well-being in pursuit of one's own interests exemplifies the underlying component of moral harm that distinguishes it from other forms of injury.

This comparison underscores the unique and insidious nature of moral harm. The damage extends beyond the physical or emotional; it lies in the deliberate disregard for basic safety and human dignity, striking at the very core of one's sense of worth. The intentional nature of the act compounds the harm exponentially, leaving a lasting imprint on the survivor's sense of self.

Moral harm is not confined to severe cases; it permeates daily life in smaller, less overt ways. We might treat a waiter with contempt when service doesn't meet our expectations, yell at a driver who we feel could be driving better, or scheme to get ahead at work at a colleague's expense. These moments of disregarding another's basic dignity because our desires are unmet are less severe examples of moral harm but harmful nonetheless.

The degree of harm varies based on the extent of the damage, the pervasiveness of the behavior, and the level of responsibility we attribute to the offender. Complex factors influence an offender's choices, including their understanding of their actions, the power they hold over the harmed person, and their intentions.

The Role of Justification in Moral Harm

Sexually harming another person often involves self-deception or justification on the part of the offender, a mechanism to ward off their own shame. This process frequently includes degrading the victim to rationalize harmful actions or shifting blame onto the victim or others. This dynamic is not limited to the offender; those close to the situation often engage in similar justifications, contributing to a culture of denial and minimization.

Most of us intuitively understand the wisdom of the golden rule: "Do unto others as you would have them do unto you." This ethic of reciprocity transcends individual moral codes and binds us as a collective humanity. When someone exploits another person they deem "lesser" to serve their own interests, it distorts this shared understanding, provoking an innate sense of injustice.

Similar to a schoolyard bully or an overbearing boss, those who disregard the basic dignity of others violate an unspoken social covenant. Such behaviors often elicit widespread condemnation for failing to meet our collective moral compass. This reaction is especially pronounced in public responses to child sexual abuse, where moral harm is not an abstract concept but the lived experience of dehumanization. Acts that disregard another's humanity leave an indelible mark, one that is not easily integrated into the survivor's life. A sense of "less worth" often takes root, even if it manifests outwardly as independence, confidence, or defiance. Being treated as a means to someone else's end fundamentally disrupts the development of intrinsic worth—a basic building block of a well-functioning adult.

Understanding moral harm deepens our appreciation for the long-lasting effects of child sexual abuse, allowing us to approach both survivors and those who caused harm with a better understanding of the true nature of the injury. Only by addressing moral harm at its root can we begin to foster healing within individuals, families, and communities.

Understanding the Shame Event

The impact of moral harm is driven by the shame it produces. Shame is not just a feeling but an immediate, visceral reaction to the violation of a moral code. It is the intolerable experience of feeling socially threatened, as if our place in the world is at risk, especially in our most important relationships.

A "shame event" occurs when someone disregards the humanity of another triggering a surge of shame. It is an immediate reaction to the mistreatment that bypasses the conscious mind, activates our survival instincts and causes us to involuntarily push away from the painful experience.

The deep-seated feelings of unworthiness, brokenness, or contamination resulting from shame events generate such intensity that individuals instinctively distance themselves from these emotions, often for extended periods. This distancing from our own lived experiences arises, often beyond our conscious control, as a means of coping with the fear resulting from moral harm.

Shame manifests internally in various ways: a sense of internal collapse, self-loathing, disconnection from others, or a feeling of invisibility. It can also provoke outward expressions such as an unwillingness to depend on others, an intense vigilance, anger, defensiveness, or aggression. These primal, unconscious reactions occur quickly, often before the individual can fully process or make sense of the situation that is triggering them.

As inherently social beings, we are wired to avoid shame and the situations that cause it. It signals a threat to our social connections and therefore our safety, especially when we are young. Whether we are the recipient of the mistreatment, the offender, or a bystander, moral harm triggers an intense and immediate response in everyone, highlighting the power it has to shape us.

From Adaptive to Maladaptive

Shame, in its intended form, is not inherently harmful. It serves a crucial function in human relationships, acting as an internal alarm system that helps us navigate our place in the community. It alerts us when we have acted in ways that threaten social bonds, signaling that a course correction is needed. This discomfort can prompt self-reflection, encourage repair when we have wronged someone, and reinforce the behaviors that sustain trust and belonging.

Shame can also be protective. It alerts us when we are being mistreated, sparking an instinct to push back against those who cross our boundaries. In this way, it serves as a regulating force, guiding both individual behavior and communal expectations. Healthy shame keeps relationships balanced, fosters accountability, and ultimately strengthens the social fabric.

However, when the intensity is high, it can be quite destructive to an individual, especially true for young people. Child sexual abuse is a violation so profound that it overwhelms the normal function of shame. Sexual harm against a child is deeply destabilizing—not only for the survivor but for those around them.

It can disrupt the social order, confronting families and communities with something too painful to face directly. The weight of this shame can feel unbearable, leading people to turn away from the reality of what has happened rather than confront it.

For the child, this response is devastating. When adults signal, explicitly or implicitly, that the harm is too shameful to acknowledge, the child is left to absorb the shame alone. Without guidance to process what has happened, they may internalize a sense of unworthiness, believing the violation says something about who they are rather than what was done to them. Over time, this misplaced blame distorts their self-perception, shaping how they see themselves, others, and their place in the world.

Families, too, struggle under the weight of this shame. Instead of holding space for the child's pain, they may distance themselves emotionally, minimize the harm, or even deny it altogether. Their own unresolved trauma—whether from this event or past wounds—can make it impossible for them to support the child or young person in the way they need.

When shame functions as it should, it fosters accountability, boundary-setting, and repair. But when it becomes entangled with a high degree of trauma, it loses its ability to guide us toward healing. Instead, it fuels isolation, self-blame, and cycles of avoidance that can persist for a lifetime. The challenge, then, is to disentangle shame from the harm itself, helping survivors see that the violation was not a reflection of their worth but of someone else's failure to honor it.

Coping Mechanisms

A shame reaction refers to the immediate, instinctive emotional and physiological responses triggered by a shame-inducing event. These reactions often include feelings of embarrassment, humiliation, anger, or a strong desire to withdraw from the situation. They occur automatically as a defense mechanism, aiming to protect the individual from further emotional distress.

Coping mechanisms are the strategies individuals develop to manage and mitigate the lingering effects of shame. These mechanisms can be both adaptive and maladaptive, including behaviors such as denial, deflection, minimization, justification, self-blame, isolation, or dissociation. While these strategies may offer temporary relief, they can also impede long-term healing if left unexamined and unaddressed.

The progression from an initial shame reaction to the formation of coping mechanisms can lead to enduring symptoms that persist long after the original event. These long-term effects can manifest as physical illness, emotional dysregulation, difficulties in relationships, struggles with finding a balance in our adult responsibilities, and reliance on mood-altering behaviors. Such outcomes reflect the cumulative impact of the harm over time.

The Developmental Lens

For a child who experiences sexual abuse, their sense of self-worth can become deeply altered, affecting how they understand relationships and their place in the world. They may struggle with confusion about their value, safety, and ability to trust others, particularly adults. Often, children carry misplaced feelings of responsibility for the abuse or fear that disclosing it will harm their family.

Many children cope by dissociating from traumatic events, either failing to recognize them as abuse or trying to bury the memories in an effort to forget. This delayed recognition, shaped in part by the developmental stage of the brain, helps explain why children rarely disclose abuse right away. Although dissociation serves as a survival mechanism at the time, it often leaves the trauma unresolved, sometimes for decades.

The brain's development, particularly the maturation of the prefrontal cortex in the mid-twenties, plays a critical role in processing traumatic experiences. Until this cognitive capacity is fully developed, children struggle to accurately assign responsibility for the abuse. They often lack the tools to comprehend their innocence and victimization fully, making it difficult for them to articulate their feelings or experiences.

This cognitive limitation, combined with the confusion and shame surrounding the abuse, makes sexual harm against children particularly insidious and difficult to detect or report. In cases where the harm is caused by another child, the individual causing harm may eventually experience significant shame as they mature. This shame typically leads them to stop harmful sexual behaviors while they are still minors. Rarely do these children reoffend as adults, though the damage done must still be addressed.

When adults intentionally exploit children, the developmental vulnerabilities of young people tragically make sexual abuse an easier crime to commit. As adults, we must learn to overcome our own unconscious shame reactions when confronted with boundary-crossing behaviors in others. Instead of looking away or assuming good intentions, we must take it upon ourselves to address these behaviors directly and early.

As adults, our mature cognitive abilities enable us to recognize red flags and intervene on behalf of children, yet this rarely happens. Prevention requires not just knowledge of the signs of abuse but the skill to overcome our fear that to intervene in a boundary crossing will destroy our relationships, or put us in the line of fire with our community.

It also requires we have a support network who can affirm that we are, in fact, unwinding a distortion, and making a proper correction in the behavior of another. While adults have the ability to understand a harmful situation, they do not often have the emotional strength to address it.

False Allegations

A common misconception often voiced by those unfamiliar with trauma reactions is, "If the abuse really happened, why wouldn't they have said something at the time?" Or "why wouldn't you have told me if it was impacting your life in this way?" These questions reveal a fundamental misunderstanding of how shame operates, particularly in cases of sexual harm.

Shame is a forceful and painful, yet self-protective mechanism. It can silence individuals, especially those who were directly harmed, preventing immediate confrontation or disclosure of abuse. For individuals under twenty-five years old, whose prefrontal cortex—the area of the brain responsible for decision-making and understanding long-term consequences—is still developing, silence is an understandable response to trauma. Fault for not speaking up immediately after experiencing harm fails to acknowledge the often nonlinear, time-consuming journey of battling the shame event long enough to see one's innocence.

The average age at the time of disclosure is 52 years old, and in only a small fraction of cases is harm reported to an adult during childhood. It is typically only later in life, as survivors gain self-determination, personal power, and emotional maturity, that they begin to address their past experiences. Slowly, survivors begin to recognize and understand the patterns left in the wake of their abuse. This delayed recognition is not a sign of fabrication but a common and natural part of the healing journey for most survivors.

Moreover, statistics offer important context. Around 20% of the global population will experience sexual abuse before the age of 18. The vast majority of those incidents (88%) will go unreported to the authorities. Of the 12% that are reported to authorities, research suggests that around 2-10% are credible situations of false allegations, many of which arise in the context of custody disputes. Recognizing the small fraction of cases where the allegation is false, and the monumental number of cases per year worldwide that go unreported, is helpful when we find ourselves denying harm, ours or someone else's.

Jake's Story

Jake's world fractured the day his parents divorced, leaving him adrift in a sea of uncertainty. At seven years old, he was in a new home, watching his mother build a life with a man whose eyes rarely left the TV screen or his phone. Jake, shy and unsure, felt like a ghost in his own home, his presence barely acknowledged.

The sound of his mother's key in the lock each evening brought a fleeting hope of connection. As she burst through the door, a whirlwind of energy and words to her new husband, Jake found himself pushed to the periphery once again. He'd hover at the edges of his mother and stepfather's animated conversations, straining to insert himself into their plans, only to realize most of their excitement centered around the weekends when he'd be away at his father's.

Weekends with his dad were his lifeline. In his father's house, Jake wasn't invisible; he was the sun around which everything revolved. Every moment was filled with adventure and laughter - ballgames, movie marathons, visits with friends. His father's undivided attention made Jake feel seen, loved, whole. In those precious hours, Jake's heart opened in the warmth of his father's affection.

When the sun started to go down, the sound of running water from the shower became a harbinger of dread. His father would call to him to get undressed and get into the shower before bed in a voice that had changed in some almost imperceptible way.

An insidious wrongness distorted the room's atmosphere. Jake would squeeze his eyes shut, his small body rigid with fear, silently pleading, 'Oh no, not again.' His father whispered assurances of love in his ear as Jake stood naked and vulnerable, his gaze fixed on the floor.

Morning would bring a cruel reset. As the aroma of sizzling eggs filled the air, accompanied by his father's cheerful whistling, Jake struggled under the weight of memories that were already slipping away. The night before felt like a fading nightmare, leaving behind only a vague sense of unease.

His father's voice, bright with excitement, cut through the fog: "The neighbor got a new puppy! Want to go see? Maybe we could get one too!" And just like that, the last wisps of the previous night evaporated, replaced by a genuine smile. The promise of a puppy, the infectious joy in his father's voice - it was all so wonderfully normal, being loved.

Years passed, and Jake built a life of his own, complete with a loving wife and a son who was the spitting image of himself at that age. As his boy approached his seventh birthday, something dark began to stir in Jake's subconscious. Anger, long suppressed, began to bubble to the surface. Memories, once carefully locked away, started to assault him in vivid flashbacks.

One ordinary evening, as Jake's wife called their son for his bath, the simple sound of running water catapulted Jake back to his childhood trauma. His body began to shake uncontrollably and he started to scream to his wife to turn off the water! Annoyed, she turned it off and gave her son a shallow bath. By the time his wife returned from tucking their son in, she found Jake curled up on the floor, sobbing.

"What happened?" she asked, her voice laced with concern and confusion. She had never seen her husband this way. But Jake, still lost in the whirlpool of resurfacing memories and emotions, could only shake his head. "I don't know," he choked out, as flashes intruded into his mind. He loved his dad. He was the lifeline to his whole life. After an hour or so, he was calm again. When she sat down to hear what had happened, he changed the subject.

They never spoke of it again.

Jake's story illustrates the complex interplay between love, abuse, and shame. It demonstrates how shame can suppress memories and delay the recognition of harm. Often, it's the triggers or unexplained negative symptoms—physical, emotional, relational, or an inability to function like one's peers—that bring the past to the surface.

Shame has an extraordinary ability to keep abuse hidden, sometimes for a lifetime. It can suppress traumatic events, burying them just below the surface of awareness. While this defense mechanism allows individuals to function, it often comes at a steep emotional cost. It protects the mind until the person is better prepared to confront the pain though for some, that moment may never come.

Our Offending Loved One

When the person who has caused sexual harm is someone we love, it can create an unbearable conflict. Families often feel trapped between two extremes: either fully confronting the harm and severing ties, or denying it altogether to preserve the relationship and the community surrounding them. This false choice leaves many unable to take meaningful action. Survivors, sensing the weight of this tension, may choose silence to avoid further disruption. When the truth can not be pushed down any longer, it inevitably shifts the family system, forcing relationships to realign.

It is possible to hold both truths at once—to acknowledge the seriousness of the harm while also recognizing the humanity of the person who caused it. There is a middle path, one that neither dismisses nor exiles, but instead pulls the person who caused harm into the fold with accountability and support. This does not mean forcing reconciliation on the survivor, nor does it mean shielding the offender from the natural consequences of their actions. Instead, it is about offering a framework for accountability and repair, guiding them toward the deep internal work required to take responsibility.

It is important to recognize that this process is not the survivor's burden to carry. Forgiveness is a personal choice, and no one is entitled to it. However, there are often other family members who are uniquely positioned to hold the person who caused harm accountable while also showing them the steps toward healing. These individuals can help ensure that accountability is not about punishment, but about meaningful change.

To support a loved one who has caused harm, we must first process our own emotions of rage, disappointment, grief, and fear, in our own safe space away from the family. Only after working through these feelings can we engage from a place that is both clear-eyed and constructive. The reality of what has happened cannot be changed, but how we respond to it has the power to shape the future.

We often assume that confronting someone who has harmed must be fueled by rage, rejection, and judgment. But shame and isolation rarely lead to transformation. When approached with compassion and clear expectations, accountability has the power to create real change. A loved one's support can be the difference between someone avoiding responsibility and actively working to make amends, whether to the person they harmed, the family as a whole, or society in general.

The Long-Term Effects on Families

To those outside the family, the lingering effects of sexual harm can seem baffling. How can someone stay married to a person who sexually abused their child? Why would a survivor maintain ties with family members who protected the abuser? Why would someone who was harmed by a parent allow that parent to care for their own children unsupervised? These choices seem incomprehensible unless we understand how shame distorts perception, reshapes loyalties, and binds families together in complex ways, even when harm has occurred.

Healing requires more than addressing individual harm. It involves creating an environment where the family as a whole can confront moral injury, cope with its impact, and rebuild trust. This is difficult because 'group think' often takes precedence over emotionally trying truth, and the need to preserve family bonds can override the instinct to protect those who have been harmed. Even survivors, as adults, may struggle to fully break free from these patterns, finding themselves pulled back into the same harmful dynamics they once endured.

Shame influences not just individual coping mechanisms but the entire family system, shaping narratives that justify, minimize, or obscure harm. Denial may be framed as keeping the peace, silence mistaken for strength, and self-sacrifice seen as loyalty. For example, participating in the wedding party of the person who caused sexual harm, saying nothing to the new spouse about the past.

Escaping these cycles often requires stepping outside the family system, at least temporarily. When survivors or family members seek support beyond the distortions of their upbringing, they gain the clarity and strength to dismantle the coping mechanisms that once felt necessary for survival. This is exponentially harder for those who remain enmeshed in the family, where triggers are constant and the pressure to conform remains strong.

While individual growth is powerful, change accelerates when multiple family members commit to unraveling unhealthy dynamics together. When more than one person names the harm, questions the family's silence, or refuses to participate in distorted narratives, the weight of secrecy begins to lift. Collective truth-telling weakens shame's grip, making room for real healing to take hold.

This work is neither easy nor linear. It requires compassion, patience, and an unyielding commitment to truth. By refusing to turn away from harm and confronting the forces that allow it to persist, families have the potential to rebuild trust and connection for all.

CHAPTER 6

The Spirit in Words

Language can be a powerful tracker of how both individuals and societies evolve. Take the word "woke" as an example. Not long ago, it referred to a newly awakened awareness of systems of oppression. Over time, it became shorthand for a general kind of social consciousness. Then it took a sharp turn. Now used to mock people seen as overly sensitive or politically correct.

Eventually, it became a catch-all term for DEI policies, laced with sarcasm and eventually extreme hostility toward any effort to acknowledge difference. Today, I no longer use the word because I'm not sure what it means anymore, to me or to the person hearing it.

That is the point: words bend and change. They carry different meanings over time, depending on who's using them, how, and why. Even in their instability, words can be sturdy vessels for our inner experiences and common bridges to being understood, if we hold them as temporary, flexible, and personal.

When someone finds language that captures a lived experience, especially one paired with a newfound insight, that moment can be transformative. It's a rung on the ladder of self-awareness. It is potentially a way out of isolation and into connection. When that expression is met with acceptance for one's subjective reality, without judgment, it can open space for healing.

We must resist the temptation to fix words in place and to assume that a word used once to describe someone's experience will define them forever. Words aren't meant to be permanent labels. They lose resonance when overused or clung to past their usefulness. Like scaffolding, they support our growth but are not the growth itself.

As we explore the language of healing, be curious. When someone uses a word to describe their self-awareness, listen for what they're trying to show us about their internal world. Let words be movable, changeable, temporary shelters without getting caught on the word choice. They are just ways of making meaning in the moment. Honor their utility without requiring permanence or universal definitions.

Reclaiming language in this way helps ground us on the healing path. We must be known by ourselves to heal, and we must have words, imperfect as they are, to describe how our lives occur to us.

Let's begin with the most obvious word: ***Victim***.

I personally love the word *victim*.

For many of us who have sexual abuse in our personal history, there comes a moment in recovery when our eyes widen and we realize, often with a mix of shock and recognition: *the word victim describes me*.

No one aspires to victimhood. The realization is rarely joyful but it can be a relief. To finally reach a point where we can say, *something happened to me, and it changed the course of my life*, marks a turning point. What once felt like someone else's sad story becomes unmistakably our own.

We pass through the fog of confusion or denial and recognize that we belong to a group we never wanted to join—those who carry the burden of having had their agency taken in such a way they were never quite the same again. And with that realization comes access to a body of knowledge that only those who have lived through it can truly understand.

Paradoxically, claiming the identity of *victim* can be empowering. Like receiving a long-sought diagnosis for a mysterious illness, the word provides context. It doesn't erase the pain, but it brings clarity and with that, a path forward. Naming it helps explain the symptoms we have been blaming ourselves for. And in naming it, some self compassion seeps in.

This acknowledgment is often a milestone in recovery. It offers a framework others have walked before us, one that can be studied, supported, and shared. When someone who has long minimized or denied their trauma reaches the point of embracing the word *victim*, it marks a meaningful shift. A private knowing becomes something that can be spoken aloud and, in time, witnessed and validated by others.

This stage can be difficult for families. To them, it may feel like things are getting worse. This discomfort is normal, but the word *victim* is not regression—it's progress. Healing often follows an inverted bell curve: the deeper we go into the truth, the more painful it may become before things start to feel better. The surfacing of grief, anger, or disorientation doesn't mean we're breaking down, it means we are breaking through.

The word *victim* becomes a beacon in that process. It draws us out of isolation and into connection. In hearing our own pain reflected in others, we begin to shed the weight of self-recrimination. In its place, we see a glimmer of self-compassion. It's a small but radical shift in perspective; one that allows us to view our story not through the lens of shame and guilt, but through a more nuanced understanding.

Yes, *victim* is a loaded, sometimes very scary word. It invites us to confront the uncontrollable events that shaped our lives and to examine how they've influenced our choices, relationships, and sense of self.

These experiences leave subtle, persistent, and often unspoken fractures. Tracing them, naming them, and working through the pain they carry is essential before we can begin to let go of the identity of *victim* and step into what comes next.

There is life beyond this word, this experience. As shame and secrecy begin to lift, we gain the ability to speak openly about our past without apology or fear of judgment. We stop hiding and start insisting that those close to us understand the whole truth of who we are. This is not just a personal transformation; it's a reclamation of our voice, our story, and our wholeness. It is the beginning of a more integrated, authentic life which brings us to the next word.

From the ashes of victimhood emerges a new word: *Survivor*.

This word is a battle cry, a declaration of resilience that refuses to be silenced. It's a container that expands with each retelling of our story, each boundary we set, each moment of anger we allow ourselves to feel. Family and friends may struggle with this transformation, unprepared for the seismic shifts in dynamics. But the survivor's journey waits for no one.

It often begins when long-held secrets become comfortably more public. As the truth comes into the open, the words gain strength and shed their shame. The survivor's voice grows louder, their choices bolder. This evolution can be messy, painful, and disruptive, and yet, often a necessary part of the journey. The survivor reshapes their world, even when it threatens all the stability of the status quo, because that is the cost of their survival.

Speaking our truth liberates us from shame's grip. Each utterance of our story chips away at self-blame, releasing a burden never meant to be ours, bringing a little more relief. Disclosures may rage like a wildfire, but even the most destructive flames clear the way for new growth. For loved ones who are supporting survivors, resist the urge to silence this awakening.

As we heal, we often discover unexpected strengths forged in our struggle. We all know the experience of how a significant loss can have unexpected positive consequences. How a heartbreak can lead to self-discovery, or how an illness can sharpen our appreciation for life. While we would never wish these experiences on anyone, nor would we want to relive these experiences ourselves, we recognize their profound influence on who we have become. These unwelcome teachers have sculpted us, etching wisdom into our life.

Surviving itself is a triumph over the silent deaths, literally and figuratively, experienced by those harmed by sexual abuse. The survivor's healing journey can be a tempest, forcing those around them to run for cover. Hear me smiling, as I ask loved ones to weather this storm with patience. In time, its fury will subside, leaving behind a landscape where joy and hardship can coexist.

The goal, like with the word *victim*, is not to forever wear the *survivor* badge on our chest. We are infinitely more than our trauma. Eventually, we lay down this hard-won identity. After transforming survival's fierce energy into the gentle wisdom of an elder who has walked through fire, we emerge scarred but whole.

The phrase *Those Who Have Caused Harm* leaves room for the person to be more.

Finding words to describe those who have caused sexual harm to a young person without diminishing their humanity is challenging. While terms like "perpetrator" and "offender" can be accurate, they may also hinder the path to accountability and the necessary connection that goes with it. We aim to balance compassion with responsibility when using words to describe this experience. Remembering that these too are temporary stops along the healing path. We want to invite the human being to hold the impact of their actions without losing themselves.

Let's broaden our perspective. The capacity to cause harm, driven by selfish motives or misguided actions, exists within all of us to varying degrees. While child sexual abuse is an egregious form of harm, recognizing our shared potential for hurting others can foster empathy and humility. This isn't about equating all harms, but understanding that the journey of taking responsibility and making amends is a universal human experience.

Healing from having caused any form of harm to another requires facing the impact of our actions without seeking refuge in excuses. This level of remorse and accountability is challenging, often requiring support and time to develop. Shame will inevitably trigger defensiveness, pushing us to explain away our actions rather than sit with the discomfort they produce. However, it's precisely this willingness to confront the harm we have caused that paves the way for meaningful change and repair.

To those who have caused sexual harm and are reading this book: Thank you for being here. I believe we can not eradicate sexual harm without those who have caused it joining us on this healing path. Redemption is not possible without a community joining in, and while all healing is difficult, healing from causing sexual harm is absolutely possible when done together.

Problematic Sexual Behavior in *Young People*:

Sexual harm involving minors must be taken seriously and understood as fundamentally different from harm caused by adults. While the impact on the victim is not different and can be just as severe, the context often includes family dynamics, developmental differences, and power imbalances that require a distinct approach for addressing the young person who caused the harm.

When a young person causes sexual harm in the community, it can be difficult for the adults to untangle what happened and what to do next. Parents are often caught between the instinct to protect their child from lasting stigma and the uncertain path of how to respond responsibly. This hesitation is understandable—but when it leads to silence or inaction, it can compound the harm for the victim and their family. It may also lead the wider community to view the family as dismissive or complicit, increasing tension and fueling harmful dynamics.

When emotions are high and no clear action is seen, people in the community may resort to their own harmful behaviors, such as name-calling, spreading rumors, or sharing information with malicious intent. These responses often come from a place of justified pain, outrage, and fear. But when directed at a young person and their family, they are inappropriate and can make all children less safe by pushing the problem further underground.

When a young person causes sexual harm—whether within a family or the broader community—we need a different framework. One that fully acknowledges the seriousness of the harm without collapsing the young person's identity into labels shaped by sensationalized media or the criminal justice system. Words like monster, sexual predator, or even pedophile may reflect the pain of the moment, but they are not tools for accountability. They are weapons of isolation—and they obscure the issue rather than clarify it.

Instead of casting blame on a few individuals, we need to engage all adult community leaders around the behavior itself: what happened, what contributed to it, and what must change to prevent it from happening again. Blaming parents for missing warning signs or failing to teach appropriate boundaries may feel satisfying in the moment, but it rarely helps.

When adults lead with honesty and care for one another, they create the conditions for healing–for the victim, for the person who caused harm, and for the wider community. That includes stopping the behavior, helping the young person understand the impact of their actions, and guiding them toward long-term change. With appropriate intervention, most youth who engage in problematic sexual behavior do not go on to cause sexual harm as adults.

Those Who Harmed Sexually as ***Adults***:

We expect adults to know better. With fully developed prefrontal cortices, adults bear a heightened responsibility to protect young people from inappropriate sexual encounters. This applies whether the child is our own, a family member, a community member, or a stranger. Our responsibility extends to addressing adults in our sphere of influence who seem to be crossing boundaries, supporting them to stop, and getting help when needed.

Let's clarify the terminology surrounding this sensitive issue

> **Pedophile:** An adult primarily or exclusively attracted to prepubescent children, regardless of whether or not harm has been caused.
>
> **Hebephilia:** Sexual attraction to early adolescents, typically ages 11-14, regardless of whether or not harm has been caused.
>
> **Ephebophilia:** Sexual interest in later adolescents, approximately ages 15-19, regardless of whether or not harm has been caused.
>
> **Minor-attracted person (MAP):** A broader term encompassing pedophiles, hebephiles, and ephebophiles.
>
> **Non-offending minor-attracted person (NOMA):** Someone who experiences attraction to minors but has never harmed a child or acted on these attractions.
>
> **Child sexual offender (CSO):** An adult who has sexually abused a child, regardless of their attractions.
>
> **CSAM:** Child Sexual Abuse Material, the legally and ethically preferred term for what was previously called *child pornography*.

These terms have specific meanings that are often misused. In today's political climate, words like "pedophile" are wielded as weapons rather than used for their actual meaning. While it may feel justified to use these words as insults, we must consider our ultimate goal when addressing those who have harmed children sexually: preventing future harm and promoting genuine accountability.

Misusing these terms distorts their meaning. Most people who harm children sexually are not attracted exclusively to children. Yet when we assign the word 'pedophile' to a wide variety of behaviors, we shut down opportunities for supporting someone who is struggling to not cause harm. We risk driving the behavior underground, where it can flourish in isolation, or diluting the word's impact, potentially leading to inaction in the face of actual harm. If the connotation of the words repel the person genuinely struggling or open to being accountable from stepping forward, we all lose.

In cases of sexual assault, such as date rape, resist overly simplistic categorizations. Dividing the world into 'sexual predators' and 'the rest of us' based on an accusation oversimplifies complex societal issues. The individuals who deliberately exploit situations to sexually harm another without consent, need a specific intervention if for no other reason than to protect the rest of us. And, there are others who may genuinely misunderstand or misread signals of consent. The latter, while still harmful to the victim, presents a nuanced opportunity for intervention and education.

Team Victim v Team Offender

If we're locked into binary roles of *accuser* and *defender* in all cases, we lose chances for humane intervention at times when that would go further in accomplishing our goals. The key is to treat each situation as unique, making no excuses but focusing on: healing for all who feel harmed, meaningful accountability and an end to the problematic behavior, and prevention to increase safety in the future.

The nuance of individual cases is often lost in our criminal justice system, where the state accuses (regardless of what the victim wants or needs) and the accused defends themselves (and is not asked to be accountable or learn something, or get support to change). This is somewhat the opposite of what is needed for healing, accountability and even prevention. While this approach may be appropriate in some situations, it isn't universally applicable.

This paradigm shift will be hard-won. To prevent harm, we must create conditions where attraction to minors doesn't automatically lead to acting on those feelings. Support and intervention goes a long way in managing these attractions. We must resist jumping to conclusions about who someone is when we hear something concerning. If we opt for reserving judgment until we know more, we will not contribute to the frenzy that leads us away from a productive intervention.

Of course, there are individuals who harm sexually with full consciousness of their actions. The damage they cause is exponential knowing they consciously intend to harm others. Some may be too entrenched in their behavior by the time they're confronted to address the harm they've caused. There are people who will not be able to stop themselves from sexually harming more vulnerable people, even with the resources to get into recovery.

However, to me, it's worth creating a path to recovery for those who want it, and those who could benefit from it. Considering that more than 50% of sexual harm is caused by young people, there is reason to believe that our resources are better spent on interventions that bring about healing and meaningful accountability. By creating an alternative to the judicial or carceral model, we open space for some discernment of the individual situations.

Forgiveness Is Not the Goal

Forgiveness is not a choice we can force. It is not a decision made by the mind, but a feeling that may arise in the body, unbidden. It may find us. It may not. Either way, healing is possible. Forgiveness is not a prerequisite for peace, nor is it the destination. The true aim of healing is a return to our best self.

Well-meaning family members often urge survivors to "forgive and forget," to "move on," or to "see the good" in the person who caused harm. These pleas may come from a place of concern or love, but to a survivor, they often land as a reminder of just how alone and misunderstood they are.

If we're honest, our urge for someone to forgive often comes from our own need for relief. We want to feel like the issue is resolved; one less weight to carry, one less thing to worry about. We long for the sense of wholeness we once had, or thought we had, as a family. The dull ache that hovers over so many interactions takes effort to navigate. When family members push in different directions, tension builds. And in the midst of it all, we just want the discomfort to end.

Healing is not about restoring old family dynamics or meeting anyone else's expectations. It's about shedding the weight of shame, reclaiming one's life, and rebuilding the capacity for safe, trusting relationships. That work belongs to the survivor, the person who caused the sexual harm, and everyone else who has been impacted. We cannot outsource healing to others. We must each take responsibility for our own part of the work. What that looks like will vary depending on our role in the family and in the harm.

As supporters and loved ones, our job is not to set the pace or define the outcome. It is to walk alongside, to witness the ups and downs, to offer patience and presence, and to respect the survivor's process, however long it takes.

Forgiveness may emerge as a by-product of healing. It may never come at all. Both are valid. What matters most is that the peace we find is truly our own. Earned, not expected. Claimed, not coerced. Forgiveness, if it comes, is a gift. And forgiveness might not be part of someone's healing equation. Knowing this is also a gift.

CHAPTER 7

A Tattered Blueprint

It arrived like the proverbial message in a bottle from the other side of the world. A stapled together, bootleg photocopy of Derek Brookes' unpublished book, "Beyond Harm," smuggled to New York City by my cheeky friend Anne-Marie from Australia. An inch was cut off at the right margin, which meant inferring the last word or two of each line. It didn't matter. The teaching was evident. I devoured it almost in one sitting.

As I have mentioned before, my journey to this work was both unexpected and predestined. The book's wisdom pierced through a veil I didn't even know was there, illuminating why child sexual abuse left such enduring scars that had defied years of therapy.

Inspired by the writings, I sketched a simple three-step framework on newsprint. It reflected what I was learning from Brookes, aligned with my own insights about why I, and so many others I knew, struggled to fully heal from sexual harm experienced in youth. It was a very basic, step-by-step way to explain the path to healing.

It wasn't a magic formula; healing is never linear in the way I drew it. However, seeing my lived experiences laid out so simply brought an unexpected sense of clarity and control. The years of internal and relational conflict, and the deep stuckness I had carried for decades suddenly explained in a logical way gave me relief. For the first time, I could see the shape my trauma had taken and could imagine the way through it.

In 2016, I gathered eight friends who had also experienced sexual harm in their childhood. Crowded around the table in my not so large office, with the newsprint sketch taped to the wall, something remarkable happened. Over the weeks we met, that simple framework gave us structure. As we worked through it in the context of our own lives, it slowly became our north star.

It helped us give voice to our lived experiences in new ways. The framework supported us in articulating what had often felt inexpressible. It illuminated our own behaviors and those of the people around us, unraveling long-held knots of confusion and pain. In its simplicity, it brought new insight and, unexpectedly, compassion to ourselves, to each other, and even to the people in our lives that had been hurting us.

For 12 weeks, we shared our stories. Speaking our truths in the company of others who had lived through similar experiences made us feel truly seen. Listening to each other brought a profound sense of relief. There was no therapist, no facilitating expert. Just allies, creating a space where understanding came not from theory, but from lived experience. We didn't receive pity; we felt anger, solidarity, and strength. It was empowering, like breaking out of an invisible prison.

Looking back, I'm proud of what we accomplished. It wasn't easy. Emotions ran high, symptoms flared up, adding to our already very busy lives. Some of us returned to therapy after many years. Others were forced to address worsening physical issues. Despite the activation and amidst the pain, healing took root in ways we had not experienced.

That tattered piece of newsprint became a silent witness to our transformations. It traveled from wall to wall for dozens, then hundreds. Eventually thousands of family members with a personal experience of child sexual abuse have worked through their own experiences using this framework. We started to call it: *The Path to Healing from Harm*. Its simplicity has remained largely unchanged a decade later, a testament to its fundamental truth.

I'm deeply grateful for Dr. Brookes' teachings, which helped spark the creation of this model. For many of us, it offered the kind of structure we hadn't found elsewhere. Every healing journey is unique, shaped by its own setbacks and progress, but having a shared understanding and language made it possible to locate ourselves in the process and to keep going.

Healing isn't about erasing the past; it's about learning to live with it differently. What follows is the model that emerged from those early conversations: a path shaped by experience, reflection, and the hope that none of us has to navigate this alone.

THE PATH TO

PHASE I
Coping

Allowing our Awareness to be Limited for Our Own Protection

HEALING FROM HARM

CREATED BY ©ELIZABETH CLEMANTS 2016

PHASE II
Facing

Embracing the Awareness of the Harm and Its Impact

PHASE III
Releasing

The Shame Event Diminishes as a Defining Feature of One's Life

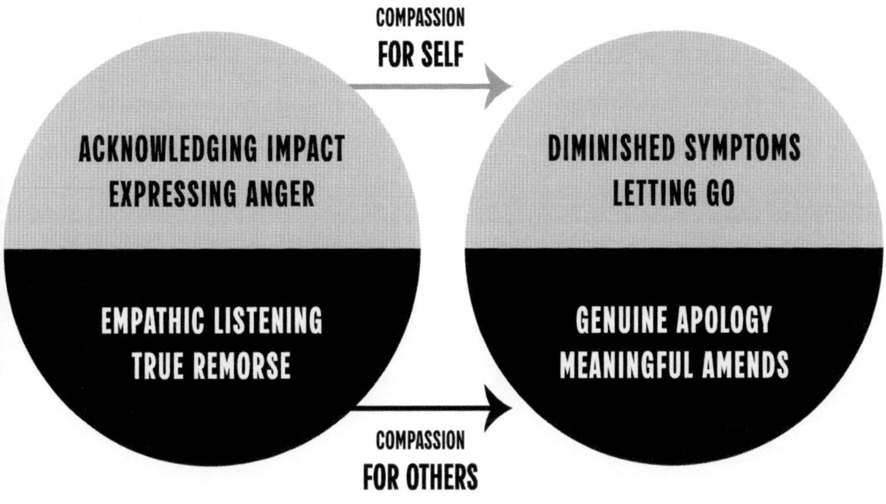

PHASE 1: LONG TERM SYMPTOMS

Trauma is a response to a deeply distressing event(s) that overwhelms a person's ability to cope. Over time, it can lead to lasting symptoms that disrupt daily life. Below is a list of some common long-term effects of trauma, often appearing in unique combinations. When they begin to interfere with a person's goals, relationships, or sense of well-being, that individual often seek help to consciously address the past trauma and its aftermath.

PHYSICAL

Back Pain
Bed Wetting
Biting Self
Brain Fog
Chronic Illnesses
Cutting
Endometriosis
Exhaustion
Fragmented Sleep
Frequent Falls
GI Issues
Headaches
Hyper-somnia
Immune Disorders
Memory Loss
Night Terrors
Pulling Out Hair
Rashes
Sleep Apnea
Sleep Disruption
Sleep Paralysis
Tired/Fatigued
Unhealthy Eating
Weight Gain/Loss

EMOTIONAL

Anger - Rage
Anxiety
Complex PTSD
Depression
Disruptive Worrying
Dissociation
Feeling Lack of Control
Feeling Like Imposter
Flashbacks
Frequent Confusion
Frequently Suspicious
Generalized Guilt
Generally Feeling Unsafe
Hyper-Focused
Hyper-Vigilant
Intrusive Thoughts
Low Self Esteem
Mania
Obsessive Thoughts
Overly Confident
Overwhelmed
Panic Attacks
Self Loathing
Suicidal Ideation
Unfocused/Distracted

RELATIONAL

Abusive Relationships

Assigning Blame

Boundary Crossing

Controlling Others

Disappearing

Disloyal Friendships

Dominating Circumstances

Expecting Others to Meet Our Needs

Frequent Conflict

Frequent Criticism

High Tolerance for Inappropriate behavior

Inability to Commit

Inappropriate Hostility

Isolating-Walling Off

Misinterpreting Intent

Multiple Short-term Partners

No Intimate Partners

Non Communicative

One-Sided Caretaking

Performative/Code Switching

Projecting onto Others

Pushing People Away

Sabotaging Self and Relationships

Seduction Bombs

Too Busy to Connect

Toxic Dynamics in Family

Untrusting/Untrustworthy

ADULT RESPONSIBILITIES

Abdicating Adult Responsibilities

Always Busy - No down time

Assuming Responsibility for Other Adults

Avoiding Typical Self Care

Catastrophizing Problems

Crushing Debt

Dependent on Parents

Frequent Work Absences

Hyper Critical of Mistakes

Not Seeking Medical Care

Over Committing to Work

Overly Concerned with Resources

Overworking

Perceived as Unreliable

Perfectionism

Under or Unemployed

Unnecessarily Defensive

Unnecessary Work Drama

Unpaid Bills/Bad Credit

Unpaid Taxes

Unstable Housing

Unwilling to Ask for Help

Volunteering to Move Mountains

MOOD ALTERING

Creating Fantasy World

Disordered Eating

Drawn to Drama/Chaos

Drawn to Toxic People

Drug Induced Apathy

Drug Induced Dysregulation

Drug Induced Rage

Excessive Exercising

Intrusive Behavior

Manipulating Others

Marijuana Dependency

Over Gambling

Over Spending

Over Use of Alcohol

Prescription Drug Misuse

Recreational Drug Misuse

Sexually Obsessive

Splitting/Creating Conflict

Unhealthy Risk-Taking

Unnecessarily Lying

Workaholic

The *Path to Healing from Harm* consists of the Shame Event, followed by three phases:

I. Coping,

II. Facing, and

III. Releasing.

Each stage represents part of the healing journey.

While it is important to note that we move back and forth through these three phases at different times, in different circumstances, and perhaps some part of us is always in each of the three phases, it is meant to simplify something infinitely complex. It is a roadmap meant to be a flexible representational guide so we might orient ourselves, take a deep breath and start again.

The Shame Event:

A *shame event* is an experience in which another person disregards our humanity, with little or no regard for how their actions will affect our overall well-being. Sexual harm is, by definition, a significant shame event. When an adult or a more powerful minor uses a young person for their own sexual gratification, it inflicts a loss that cannot easily be reclaimed. Something essential is taken, leaving a lasting impact on the person who was harmed.

The *Path to Healing from Harm* begins with that initial shame event. It also includes the aftermath of the initial harm, as our unique combination of coping mechanisms and long term symptoms are often sources of more shame. Over time, this accumulation can erode our sense of self and alter the course of our lives.

I will include a broad definition of child sexual abuse here so we are all operating from the same understanding of what is meant by sexual harm in this book.

Defining Child Sexual Abuse

Child sexual abuse encompasses any sexual activity involving a child or young person, initiated by an adult or a more powerful minor, in which the child is exploited for the sexual gratification of another person. This includes both contact and non-contact behaviors, and extends beyond what is legally defined as abuse to include a wide range of coercive, manipulative, or exploitative actions that cause harm, whether physical, emotional, or psychological.

Sexual abuse includes, but is not limited to:

Contact behaviors: Any form of unwanted or inappropriate touching; oral, vaginal, or anal penetration (including with objects); or forcing or persuading a child to engage in sexual acts.

Non-contact behaviors: Exposing a child to sexual activity or pornography, voyeurism (watching a child in private settings), sexual harassment, exhibitionism (exposing oneself), or sexualized communication.

Sexual abuse through technology: Includes sextortion, catfishing, coercing or tricking a child into sending sexual images or videos, deepfakes, sharing or trading sexually explicit material of minors, and other forms of digital manipulation.

Teen sexual assault or rape: Forcing or coercing a peer into sexual activity through pressure, manipulation, threats, or shaming—even when both parties are minors. This includes cases where a young person says "no" where consent is gained through fear or guilt, or taking advantage of someone who is intoxicated, asleep, or otherwise unable to give informed consent.

Drug-facilitated assault: Using substances (such as Rohypnol/"roofies") or alcohol to lower a young person's ability to resist or consent.

Sexual exploitation: When adults or more powerful minors benefit financially or socially from the sexualization of children. This includes parents or caregivers who allow or encourage their child to be filmed or engaged sexually by others for money, or who promote their child's sexualized content online to benefit financially or in other ways.

Third-party coercion: Involving a child or teen in creating sexual content for an adult or others, even if the initial act appears consensual. For example, a teen may be coerced into filming themselves or others under the influence of an adult who profits from or distributes the content.

Harm can take many forms. It may involve physical violations, emotional manipulation, psychological trauma, or spiritual damage. It often includes betrayal of trust, shame, and a loss of agency. Penetration does not need to involve a penis—any object inserted into any orifice without consent constitutes a rape.

Importantly, child sexual abuse is not defined only by age or legality, but by power dynamics, coercion, and disregard for a child or adolescent's ability to give informed, voluntary, developmentally appropriate consent. Even when the child does not immediately recognize the experience as abuse, the long-term consequences can be deeply harmful.

Age-Appropriate Relationships

A commonly referenced formula for evaluating age-appropriate romantic or sexual relationships is:

> **Take the older person's age, divide it by two, and add seven.**
>
> *Example:*
> *A 40-year-old should not date anyone younger than 27 (40 ÷ 2 + 7 = 27).*

This is not a legal rule but a social guideline for gauging age disparities, especially when power imbalances or developmental gaps may be present. Relationships outside of this range, especially when involving minors, are often considered **age-inappropriate** and may increase the risk of coercion, manipulation, or harm.

Phase I: Coping - Protecting Ourselves

Our coping mechanisms are as unique to us as our fingerprints. They form the invisible armor we carry after a shame event. They protect us physically, emotionally, relationally, sexually, psychologically, and spiritually. These responses are not signs of weakness, but evidence of the mind's ability to shield us until we're ready to face what happened.

In the immediate aftermath of harm, we often rely on quick, reflexive strategies: *denial, deflection, minimization, justification, blaming the victim, or defending the offender*. These are protective in the short term, helping us create distance from overwhelming feelings and the rupture of trust. As we continue to use these forms of survival over longer periods of time, they lose their effectiveness. More entrenched symptoms begin to appear.

These long-term coping mechanisms often fall into five categories:

Physical
Such as: chronic pain, fatigue, or health issues

Emotional
Such as: anxiety, depression, dissociation

Relational
Such as: difficulty trusting others

Adult responsibilities
Such as: challenges with work, or meeting basic needs

Mood-altering behaviors
Such as: addictions or escapism

These symptoms differ from person to person, shaped by individual temperament, support systems, and the nature of the harm. They all serve the same purpose: to protect us from feelings we are not yet ready to face.

I've come to see these responses as a built in survival toolkit we are glad to have. They are evidence of the incredible resilience of the body, mind, and spirit. They buy us time. They carry us forward until we find more solid ground.

Eventually, though, the effort required to maintain them becomes too great. And that's when a shift begins. The coping strategies that once protected us start pointing us toward something else. We reach a crossroads where the pain of avoiding the shame event begins to outweigh the fear of facing it.

This is the threshold between surviving and healing. It marks the end of Phase I and the beginning of the next phase: *facing the harm*.

As these short term symptoms evolve into long-term ones. As our ways of coping intensify over time, they are actually heralding a new phase. They're telling us we're approaching a crossroads where facing the harm, as daunting as it seems, is becoming easier than the exhausting work of not facing it.

Phase II: Facing the Harm

Facing the harm is the turning point—the moment we stop simply enduring and begin refusing to live under the weight of what happened. This stage is rarely straightforward. It's a reckoning, a resistance, and the means for transformation.

For anyone affected by sexual abuse, whether directly or indirectly, this is where we step into discomfort on purpose. We acknowledge what got us through: the strategies we relied on, the time we needed to survive, and the distance we kept from the shame event(s). Now, we turn toward what we've avoided. We stop shaping ourselves around the pain and begin reshaping the pain itself.

This means confronting what happened, plainly and without flinching. Grief, rage, confusion, fear and other long-buried emotions surface. It's not about indulging them, but about making room for them. There are memories that have waited their turn to come up to our consciousness. We let them. What once protected us now starts to get in the way.

At this stage, things often intensify before they shift. We may feel flooded, shaken, or more reactive. That doesn't mean we're going backward. It's part of the process. We move in cycles—stepping in, pulling back, stepping in again. Each round builds our tolerance and deepens our capacity to move forward.

Over time as we face the impact of the harm, shame begins to loosen. It stops being the lens through which we understand ourselves. In its place, we gain traction, a clearer sense of choice, and firmer boundaries. There is a new kind of safety that started on the inside and now slowly reaches outward.

This isn't about reliving the trauma. It's about reclaiming what we lost alongside it. Our voice, our strength, our clarity, and other parts of ourselves can be recovered. When we face the past on our own terms, we strip it of its power to define us. What follows isn't a return to who we were, but the creation of something new.

Phase III: Releasing the Intensity

Releasing the intensity of harm and healing is a welcome point in the work we have been doing. As compassion sets in, we find the calm after the storm. It is a subtle noticing, marked by a gradual easing of the inner turmoil that once dominated our lives. The chaos produced by our symptoms begins to quiet, and we start to experience moments of unexpected clarity. Daily life takes less energy and it occurs to us that we are okay.

This isn't about hollow declarations of forgiveness or pretending the harm never happened. Significant trauma doesn't simply vanish; instead, it becomes a part of our story rather than its defining feature. We begin to realize we have some control over how this chapter influences the rest of our narrative.

These moments of releasing are not about forgetting or erasing the past. It's about integration. The harm no longer dictates our every move or reaction. Instead, it becomes a source of hard-won wisdom and, sometimes, unexpected strength. This phase is less of a final destination, and more of a new way of navigating life. We can't force it or rush it. It unfolds in its own time, teaching us to coexist with our past rather than be controlled by it.

We can recognize this phase when we notice moments of ease in our day. The constant anxiety subsides, if only briefly. We feel less compelled to control everything and everyone around us. A sense of peacefulness settles over us, maybe just for an hour. We sigh and notice the beautiful day before rushing off to our next appointment. These moments don't last forever. However, they are sign posts letting us know we are making progress.

It's all part of the process. When we do find our way back to this calmer state, it lasts a little longer. We start to lock in that feeling and we start to trust that it belongs to us. We learn to access it more often. In this way, the path becomes more familiar, and we walk it with increasing confidence.

Releasing the shame event is about holding two truths at once: acknowledging our past harm while refusing to let it dictate our future. It's accepting our history while allowing ourselves to envision and create something new. Even with our scars, our hard-earned wisdom starts to shine through.

Humans hurt each other—always have, probably always will. You, me, everyone we know, and everyone we'll never meet. We all have the capacity to cause harm, to be harmed, and to repair what's been broken. What we've lost is the roadmap.

These are the three phases of *The Path to Healing from Harm*. It's an old map and it lives in our bones. And we can still follow it to the end.

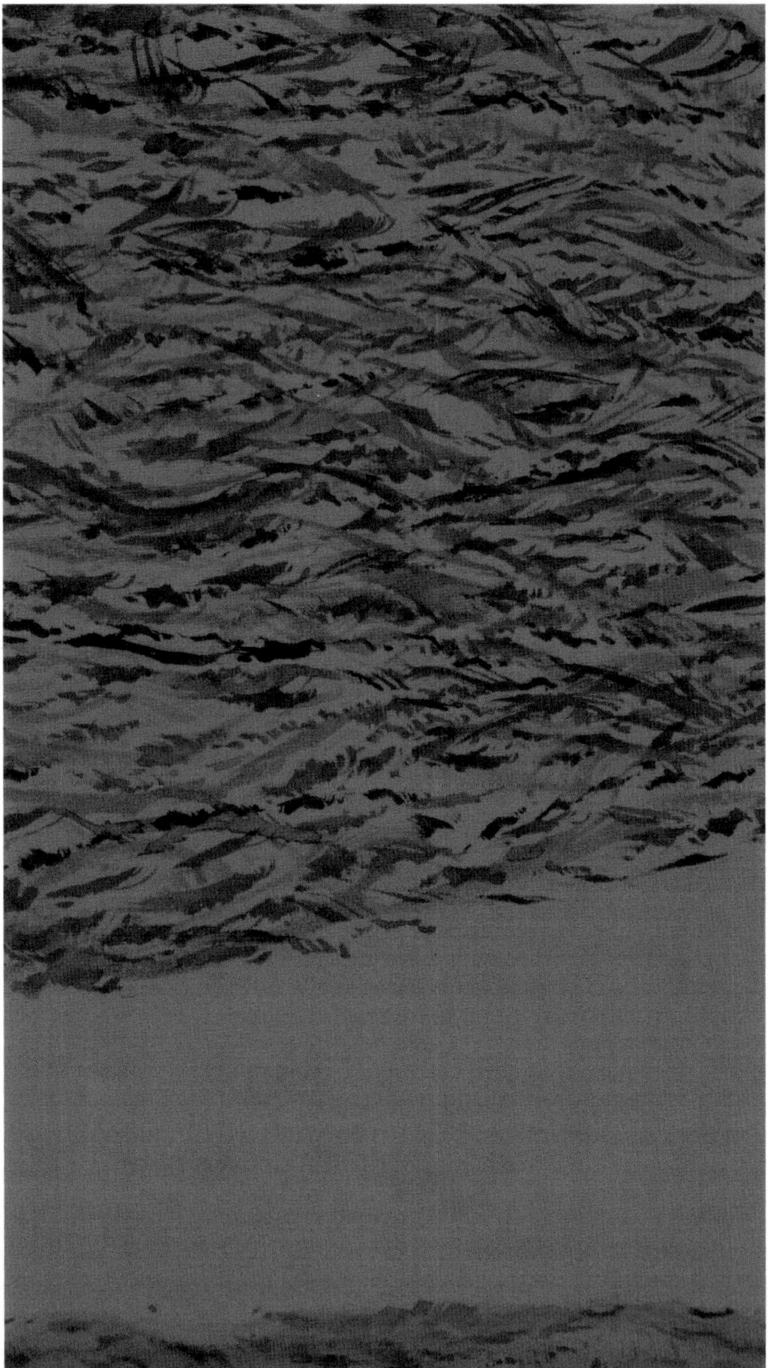

PART III

CHAPTER 8

Coping: Protecting Ourselves

Deny-Deflect-Minimize-Justify-Blame the Victim-Defend the Offender

I say these words together so often, they start to sound like one word. In fact, it is just one concept, regardless of which one of these shame reactions we employ. The very human reaction to hearing about or being involved in sexual harm is to move away from it. In our work we sometimes call this the *ICK FACTOR*, the intense emotional retreat most people have when hearing about sexual harm to a vulnerable young person.

> "Elizabeth, my sixteen-year-old daughter just told me my father molested her when she was a child. My beloved sweet father! How is it possible? What should I do?"
>
> **Answer:** "Whatever you do, resist the temptation to *Deny-Deflect-Minimize-Justify-Blame the Victim-Defend the Offender*. Stay in the moment with your daughter, and worry about integrating your thoughts about your own father later. She is the priority."

> "Elizabeth, thank you for being on our podcast to talk about the devastating impacts of child sexual abuse. Tough topic. What is the one thing people should know?"
>
> **Answer:** "Whenever you hear about a personal account of sexual abuse, whether that is told to you by the person themselves or by someone else, or even if you hear about it in the media, guard against your natural tendency to... *Deny-Deflect-Minimize-Justify or Blame the Victim-Defend the Offender.*
>
> "Elizabeth, I was just confronted by my ex (teenage) girlfriend about something I did to her two decades ago. She is threatening a civil suit against me. What should I do?"
>
> **Answer:** "The path to healing from having harmed another starts by committing yourself to holding onto your humanity while also not trying to escape to the protective place of *Deny-Deflect-Minimize-Justify-Blame the Victim or Defend* (in this case) *Yourself*. Remember that intention and impact are different. If possible, sit and listen for the impact without overlaying her experience with your intentions at the time."

I first encountered this grouping of words at The Meadows, a trauma treatment facility in Arizona. The speaker's words immediately resonated with me, capturing what I believed at the time to be the universal human response to shame, whether from big or small events.

These five strategies are protective shields for our psyche when overwhelmed by feelings we don't know how to process. Whether we are the one harmed sexually, the one who caused harm, or a loved one, these responses emerge involuntarily in various forms as a way to cope with truths too painful to bear.

Think of these shame reactions, especially as they evolve into coping strategies, as painkillers for a serious injury. They offer immediate but temporary relief, helping us get through difficult moments by masking deeper pain. While they help us endure, they do not heal us. These strategies allow us to cope with the immediate and long-term aftermath of trauma until we are ready to face it fully.

Loved ones affected by the harm, as well as those who have caused it, often resort to these shame reactions too. For a parent learning of their child's abuse, a partner discovering a loved one's trauma, or someone confronting their own actions, the urge to *Deny, Deflect, Minimize, Justify, Blame the Victim and/or Defend the Offender* can unconsciously take hold.

These responses stem from a basic human need to protect ourselves from pain, guilt, and the collapse of our worldview. For loved ones, it may seem easier to question or minimize the abuse than to face the overwhelming question of "what do I do now?" For those who caused harm, these strategies shield them from the crushing weight of responsibility and shame.

While these responses are necessary survival mechanisms in the moment, they have the potential to hinder healing. Not just for the person using them, but for everyone involved, especially the survivor. When these coping strategies are validated or reinforced by others, they can impede healing and harm family dynamics.

For example, if a non-offending parent attempts to deflect the pain by reminding the survivor of the good qualities of the one who harmed them, though this may be true, it often does more harm than good, likely retraumatizing the survivor instead of helping them heal.

While all family members may, at some point in their journey, say and do things that protect themselves from the shame that inadvertently hurts others, this is not the whole of who they are or who they could be. Most people are not readily equipped to manage this kind of harm. So, where possible, try not to lock in "who someone is" based on their reactions. If they are willing to learn, we want them to.

I honor these strategies for what they are: miraculous built-in survival mechanisms that take care of us in unconscious ways, even without us realizing at the time. Without them, many of us, myself included, might not have made it through our hardest moments. They hold us up when we lack the strength to confront what's happened.

These strategies help us sidestep the most intense pain when we are not ready but they do not heal us. We must see our tendency to deny, deflect, minimize, justify, blame the victim (or blame ourselves) or defend the offender (or defend ourselves) as a temporary intervention that helped us survive, be grateful for it, and then set it aside. Healing requires not only facing the ways we have pushed away the shame event when we could not cope with it, but also facing how our coping mechanisms caused their own damage to ourselves and our loved ones.

This perspective invites us to aim higher. Coping is not the destination; it is the starting point. It provides the time we need to face our pain and take the first steps toward healing. Whether as survivors, loved ones, or those taking responsibility for past harm, we must strive to move beyond mere survival to a place where we can truly thrive.

CHAPTER 9

The Tipping Point: When Coping Consumes Us

"Hold yourself back, or heal yourself back together. You decide." -Brittany Burgunder

For those of us who have been harmed sexually, healing rarely begins with a gentle nudge. It more often erupts when our coping mechanisms start to crumble. While those unconscious strategies may have gotten us through the initial years, they come with a hefty price tag. As time progresses, the toll of unresolved trauma becomes increasingly more evident.

Our bodies may revolt with unexplained ailments, our minds may engage in internal warfare, and our relationships may fracture under the weight of unspoken pain. The simple act of managing daily life can become overwhelmingly difficult. As we look back over our lives, we see patterns of intersecting dysfunction and ask ourselves, "How did it come to this?"

This is how: Our shame reactions turn into coping strategies. These strategies turn into long-term symptoms. And our symptoms become louder and harder to manage over time. As we struggle with the long-term effects of trauma, it becomes more abstract and harder to connect to the original source of our pain.

This is true for other family members too. A non-offending parent might find solace in nightly cocktails, using alcohol to beat back their anger and resentment towards a spouse who has harmed their child. The unharmed teenage sibling, sensing the unspoken tension disconnects, seeks refuge in after-school activities and part-time jobs. The offending parent grows more sullen, using anger to keep others from confronting them.

Time is an unforgiving auditor of our coping mechanisms. What began as a balm eventually becomes a burden. Our way of 'not dealing' with the problem becomes the presenting issue. Alcohol corrodes our health and well-being. Escaping into activities and ever-growing commitments turns into unrelenting stress. Anger damages our relationships, leading to isolation and depression.

We are now grappling not only with the original wound of sexual abuse but also with the collateral damage wrought by our own strategies for managing the pain. This may be compounded by the unhealthy strategies employed by our loved ones, which is also impacting our well-being.

These complex combinations of long term symptoms grow louder and more insistent until we face an ultimatum: confront the root cause of our suffering or watch life unravel thread by thread. This is the tipping point, where the cost of concealing our pain surpasses the fear of confronting it.

While not all coping mechanisms exact the same toll, they share a common truth: they are merely bandages on a festering wound. Only by facing the harm directly, however daunting, can we begin to gradually relinquish the strategies that have outlived their usefulness.

To better understand the far-reaching consequences of prolonged coping, I've categorized the long-term symptoms into five distinct areas: physical, emotional, relational, and life management and addictions.

Seeing these symptoms laid out can be both validating and overwhelming. On one hand, it can reflect our experiences and reassure us that we're not alone in our struggles. On the other, it can be deeply sobering to recognize the pervasive and lasting impact that sexual harm can have on a life over time.

As family members we must resist the temptation to start pointing out all the ways our survivor is happy, lucky or accomplished. This is our chance to take in the ways they have been negatively impacted, and acknowledge the damage the harm has unjustly caused. Not looking away is our step toward healing as a loved one or one who caused sexual harm. We must confront not just the shame event but the aftermath of it.

Survivors may see themselves reflected in various categories, their experiences a unique kaleidoscope of consequences stemming from the original shame event. Though perhaps discouraging at first, the full scope of symptoms can also be illuminating, showing the path forward by seeing the wake of impact behind us. By getting present to all of our symptoms, we begin to connect the dots between our past trauma and present challenges, paving the way with self-compassion.

Self compassion is the first step towards recovery. Each symptom identified is not a mark against us, but a signpost guiding us towards healing. It is through this recognition that we can begin to address these issues, slowly dismantling them to reveal the stronger, more authentic selves beneath.

Physical

Chronic Pain; Joint Pain; Fibromyalgia; Autoimmune Disorders; Cardiovascular Issues; Respiratory Problems; GI Issues; Unexplained Stomach Pain; Debilitating Back Pain; Muscle Fatigue; Headaches and Migraines; Memory Loss; Brain Fog; Inability to Focus; Hyper-Focused; Frequent Heart Racing; Insomnia; Nightmares/Night Terrors; Sleep

Paralysis; Sleep Apnea; Fragmented Sleep; Hypersomnia; Restless Leg Syndrome; Periodic Limb Movement Disorder; Circadian Rhythm Disturbances; Bedwetting; Panic Attacks; Skin Disorders; Sexual Dysfunction; Hair Loss; Disordered Eating; Bulimia; Anorexia; Unhealthy Weight Gain/Loss; Chronic Illnesses; Persistent Fatigue; Emotional Dysregulation; Hypervigilance; Cancer.

Emotional

Mild to Severe Depression; Mild to Severe Anxiety; Unmanageable Stress; Anger Bombs; Rage; Obsessive Thoughts; Intrusive Thoughts; Flashbacks; Suicidal Ideations; Manic Behavior; Self Loathing; Self Disgust; Low Self Esteem; Hyper Critical of Self; Unable to Focus; Easily Distracted; Unable to Articulate Feelings; Unstable Mood; Frequently Disregulated; Deep Sadness; Unyielding Grief; Overwhelming Sense of Loss; Feeling Burdened; Feeling Abandoned; Feeling Betrayed; Feeling Alone; Feeling Inauthentic; Feeling Helpless; Trapped; Unseen; Dissociating; Emotional Numbness; Debilitating Sensitivity; Impatience with Others; Easily Cry; Suspicious; Paranoia; Hypervigilance; Borderline Personality Disorder; Attachment Disorder; Somatization; Negative Outlook; Profound Guilt; Profound Shame; Inability to Feel Joy in Joyful Moments; Anger at Oneself; Difficulty Trusting Others.

Relational

Isolation; Unknowable; Controlling; Anger Bombs; Never Asking for Needs to Be Met; Insisting on One Way; Mask Wearing; Feeling Responsible for Others; Compulsive Caretaking; Overly Dependent on Others; Enmeshment; Unrealistic Expectations of Others; Finding Fault in Others; Self Blame; Not Trusting; Not Trustworthy; Avoiding Social Events; Always Socializing; Projecting Harm onto Situations; Projecting Bad Intentions onto Others; Sabotaging Relationships; No Intimate Partners; Frequent Short-Term Intimate Partners; Inability to Commit; Staying in Unsatisfying Relationships; High Tolerance for Inappropriate Behavior; Intense Friendships; Dramatic Breakups; Abusive Relationships; Drawn to Toxic Situations; Creating Toxic Dynamics with Family, Friends, Colleagues, or Other Communities; Frequent Conflicts;

Conflict Avoidant; Not Dependable; Drawn to Others Who Are Not Dependable; Lying/Omitting Information; Inability to De-escalate; Ceasing All Contact; Sexual Harm in Adulthood; Sexual Avoidance; Morphing Self to Fit In; Withdrawal; Feeling Lonely; Unable to See Other Perspectives; Self Absorbed.

Adult Responsibilities and Self Care

Living Dependent on Parents; Unstable Housing; Frequent Relocation; Underemployed; Unemployed; Inability to Maintain a Job; Perfectionism; Over Committing to Work; Overly Concerned About Resources; Not Consuming Enough Nutrients; Inability to Manage Finances; Frequent Overdue Bills; Buying Unnecessarily Without Resources; Crushing Debt; Bad Credit; Unpaid or Late Taxes; Abdicating Adult Responsibilities; Abdicating Adult Responsibilities to Others; Avoidance of Proper Medical or Dental Care; Irregularly Taking Medicine; Low Personal Hygiene; Not Addressing Mental Health Issues; Difficulty Setting Healthy Boundaries; Difficulty Advocating for One's Needs; Struggling to Commit to Events, Projects, or Plans; Catastrophizing Problems; Not Communicating Effectively with Others; Not Following Through on Commitments; Perceived as Unreliable by Others; Giving Others Wrong Impressions; Inability to Speak Honestly; Hyper Critical of Mistakes (Self and Others); Unnecessarily Defensive; Attributing Own Mistakes to Others; Defensive When Confronted; Unable to Accept Authority; Frequent Work Absences; Frequent Conflict with Colleagues or Neighbors; Unwilling to Ask for Help.

Mood Regulation

Unhealthy Use of Alcohol; Dependency on Marijuana; Overuse or Improper Use of Sleep Medication or Other Prescription Drugs; Risky Behavior with Illegal Drugs; Hypersexuality; Love Addiction; Shopping to Excess; Gambling to One's Detriment; Overworking to Exhaustion; Spending Beyond Means; Obsessively Saving; Excessively Exercising; Disordered Eating; Cutting; Overusing Stimulants; Codependency; Acting Unethically; Seeking Situations for Adrenaline Rushes; Anger Bombs; Raging or Violence; Overuse of Screens or Video Games;

Obsessively Engaging in Social Media or Technology; Excessive News Consumption; Prioritizing Work Over Health and Relationships.

B-r-e-a-t-h-e.

The weight of recognition often needs a minute to breathe and take it in. These lists reflect the complex reality of the aftermath of sexual abuse. It can be overwhelming to view it all in one place, and to see ourselves in symptoms we had not considered.

Healing requires us to spend time mapping the individual impact, unique to each person. These discoveries often span generations, asking in some families for meticulous detective work to uncover its full scope. Most often, healing needs a witness and a safe space to unpack the revelations as we come upon them.

As we approach "Facing the Harm" in the next chapter, we're not just confronting a single event, but a complex weave of harm, coping mechanisms, and their far-reaching consequences. This journey requires courage to confront our past, compassion to hold space for our pain, and resilience to move forward.

CHAPTER 10

Facing the Harm: When Awareness Ignites Insight

Healing often begins with a moment of reckoning—a crisis that shatters the fragile equilibrium we've built around secrecy and silence. At these inflection points the weight of what has been hidden becomes unbearable.

Imagine a non-offending mother getting upset at her adult son for losing yet another job. She compares him to his older brother in an unfavorable way. This sparks an increased intensity in the argument. A great flood of emotions pour from her son, resulting in his disclosure of sexual harm.

Or, a daughter, who moved half way around the world to start her adult life, slowly becoming more disconnected. When her father calls to tell her of her grandfather's death, fully expecting her to want to jump on a plane and come home, she laughs. His anger at her reaction prompts a long held secret of sexual harm.

These moments, while destabilizing for the family and the individuals, are the first steps toward breaking free from those stuck places. Regardless of how it comes about, this is a pivotal juncture. When we are called to face the truth, no matter how uncomfortable, we do.

Unburdening the ones who have been holding the secret alone for some time is a relief. Not just knowing what happened but processing it. Facing past harm is not the summit of the healing journey—it is the unveiling of the mountain itself. A barricade we were not even fully aware of. There is no easy descent awaiting us either. There is only one way forward and it is through, carving a path one painstaking step at a time.

Thinking of this journey as the job of mining, rather than a quick strike can make the task feel more manageable. There will be moments of breakthrough, offering glimpses of light and hope, interspersed with periods of rest and reflection. But make no mistake—this is hard work, demanding grit and determination. Yet, as we hone our skills in navigating the stuck places, the path becomes more manageable.

In this phase we are in search of movement, not comfort, breakthroughs, not softness; cracks in the rock that burst into new openings. Families often report a monumental shift in perspectives, during this facing period of the healing path. Things are not "better" but they are being understood in their enormity, sometimes for the first time.

Looking back at the tunnel we have carved offers its own rewards, a testament to our resilience and growth. Our efforts will also pave the way for others to follow, easing their journey through their own metaphorical mountain. While this work is deeply personal, it need not—and should not—be a solitary endeavor. Isolation, after all, is one of the demons we must face. While individual therapy offers valuable insights and support, the next level of healing comes from our collective community. While individual therapy offers valuable insights and support, the next level of healing comes from our community.

The most potent catalyst for healing is a supportive community. When we step into a space shared by others with similar experiences, we are not just finding solace; we are multiplying our resources. The insights we gain from holding space for the lived experiences of others' can illuminate blind spots in our own narrative, expanding our perspective beyond what we might achieve in the relative safety of individual therapy.

Spending time with non-family members who share similar experiences creates a collective space that serves as a training ground for healthier boundaries. In these settings, the stakes are lower, and understanding and non-judgment come naturally. We learn to honor different perspectives and experiences without absorbing them. We empathize without trying to fix it. We practice the delicate balance of holding space for others while maintaining our own. These skills become invaluable when we engage with our loved ones who are in their own varying stages of healing.

Community healing strikes at the twin demons that often plague those impacted by sexual harm: isolation and self-absorption. These forces, left unchecked, can spiral us into a vortex of dysfunction. While it is natural for a parent to retreat from friends upon learning of their child's abuse, or for a survivor to back away from loved ones to focus on themselves, prolonged isolation can be our undoing.

Nothing can erase what happened, or the pain it caused or the damage done. Every person bound for healing must walk through their own valley of discovery and rediscovery; there are no shortcuts. Yet, when we come together with others who have had a similar lived experience, we discover a compelling alchemy: a shift in perspective.

When we spend time in an intentional community focused on this experience, and we see ourselves reflected in the stories of others, free from judgment, a transformation occurs. Without conscious effort, our isolation begins to disintegrate, and our narrative expands. We move from seeing our pain as our solitary burden to recognizing it as part of a larger tapestry—one that touches our most important relationships, our work, our community, and society as a whole. In this shared space our individual struggles interweave with a greater story of collective healing and resilience.

In this phase of facing the harm the path branches into two distinct yet intertwined routes each offering a unique journey towards healing and accountability. A Green Path for those who are working through feeling harmed by the shame event(s) in a family system and a Purple Path for those who have caused harm to others either by causing sexual harm or with their coping mechanisms, or both.

The Green Path

This journey is for anyone who has been harmed or feels harmed by the aftermath of the shame event. It is not only for those who endured the sexual abuse directly but also for anyone who has felt the negative effects of harm in their own lives. The non-offending parent grappling with anger, the sibling feeling overshadowed, the spouse navigating a landscape of shattered trust with their in-laws—all have a place on the Green Path as they confront their own altered lives.

The Green Path recognizes that trauma does not exist in isolation; it threads through the entire fabric of the family and community. When we place the burden of healing solely on survivors, we distance ourselves from understanding the role each of us has to play in the process.

The Purple Path

This journey is about accountability and transformation, not only for those who have caused sexual harm but for any family member whose actions, intentional or not, have hurt others. It recognizes that in the aftermath of trauma, we may all behave in ways that cause harm, even without meaning to. The non-offending parent who initially dismissed their child's disclosure, the partner who arrives at a holiday gathering, overdrinks, and acts out their frustration indiscriminately—The Purple

Path invites us to move beyond the dichotomy of "the harmers" and "the harmed."

When we place the burden of accountability solely on one person in a family system, we distance ourselves from understanding the systemic nature of how this harm came about in the first place and all the ways we have contributed to the dysfunction afterward. This disproportionate burden becomes too heavy for one person to carry, and family healing stalls.

The Purple Path acknowledges that trauma of this magnitude does not begin and end in one point of time. It can not be contained but continuously moves outward in all directions, creating system-wide dysfunction. By sharing the accountability, we create the conditions for meaningful transformation and the collective work of healing the whole.

The Model

While our primary focus is on sexual harm to young people within family systems, these paths illuminate the way to healing from a vast spectrum of systemic harm. From the overt scars of physical abuse to the hidden battles of addiction, from the subtle erosion caused by emotional manipulation to the void left by neglect—this framework offers guidance.

Its reach extends beyond the family unit. The model has been successfully adapted to address school bullying, racial discrimination, and workplace harassment. At its core, it serves as a compass for navigating any system that has turned against itself, inviting each individual to step into their power as an agent of change.

This journey is a call to action, challenging us to see ourselves not as passive victims, bystanders, or those who have caused harm but as active participants in the healing process, capable of transforming both ourselves and the systems we inhabit. It invites an opportunity to separate the worst things we have ever done from our inherent humanity, giving us the strength to focus on true accountability and repair.

In the chapters ahead, we will delve deeper into these paths, examining the challenges they bring and the possibilities they hold. This journey isn't just about addressing the harm that has been done—it's about building something meaningful from the wisdom gained along the way. Together, we'll navigate the complexities, uncovering new ways to grow and reconnect.

CHAPTER 11

The Green Path: Acknowledging Impact and Expressing Anger

Sexual abuse within a family fractures the very core of trust and safety, a betrayal that leaves no clear path forward. Recovery from such devastation is not something we instinctively know how to navigate; most of us have no roadmap for finding our way through. *The Green Path* offers guidance—a way forward for anyone who has been negatively affected, whether directly or indirectly, by a significant shame event. It invites us to explore how these experiences have shaped our lives and to begin the work of rebuilding stability, belonging, and hope.

Sexual harm within a family system brings ongoing losses that affect many aspects of life. Moving forward requires acknowledging this wider impact of harm and recognizing that every family member must come to terms with how the abuse has shaped their experiences. Each person needs to confront and express their anger, whether directed at the offender, the circumstances, others' responses, or even themselves. When directed in healthy ways, this anger can ignite meaningful change and restoration within the family.

The Green Path is not a hierarchy of pain, and comparison has no place in healing. The impact of sexual abuse and the distortions it creates, shapes each person differently, making recovery a deeply personal journey. We don't diminish our own healing by recognizing the struggles of others, nor do we dismiss someone else's pain because our experience feels more direct. Each experience is valid. Embracing this perspective allows us to approach the family with greater self-awareness, insight, and empathy, fostering collective healing.

At its core, *The Green Path* is a journey of two key endeavors: acknowledging the impact of harm on our lives and finding healthy, constructive ways to express anger. These practices work together, not as a rigid process, but as integral parts of healing and growth. Each person's path unfolds in their own way, at their own pace, without the need for comparison or judgment.

Acknowledging the Impact

Recognizing how sexual abuse has affected our lives is a process of untangling our experiences and understanding how they were shaped by the harm. It requires us to examine its impact on our relationships, behaviors, and sense of self with unflinching honesty.

For survivors, this means confronting how the abuse has influenced our beliefs about ourselves and our ability to live the lives we might have envisioned if the harm had never occurred. For loved ones, it also involves grappling with an alternate reality, grieving what could have been, and reorganizing the history we thought we shared with our family.

Broken trust can be integrated and repaired, but only after its impact has been fully examined. We cannot work through what we do not first understand. This process of acknowledgment is one of the foundational building blocks of healing from harm.

This exploration is not about assigning blame or dwelling in brokenness. It's about bringing the abuse into the light, where its effects can be understood, deeply felt, and ultimately addressed. It's a step towards reclaiming power and agency, recognizing that while we can't change the past, we can shape our response to it and therefore our future.

The impact of sexual abuse extends far beyond the moment it occurs, creating a dividing line—life before and life after. Survivors may not always recognize this shift until they begin unpacking their experience. For both direct and indirect survivors, healing involves reexamining our family narrative to build a more accurate picture of how harm has shaped us.

This process isn't about rewriting the past or erasing the joy and connection that existed. Instead, it's about seeing our history with greater clarity—acknowledging both the harm and the love—to develop a more nuanced understanding of the dynamics that have shaped our relationships and ourselves.

Whether we unpack these experiences in therapy, with a trusted friend or mentor, in a group setting with others who share similar experiences, or privately in a journal, we need space to revisit our history with a more developed mind. With time and perspective, we can begin to see the full complexity of how sexual harm alters the course of a life.

As we confront the impact, new layers of awareness emerge, often bringing intense emotions to the surface. Long-buried shame may come into sharper focus, making it essential to move at a sustainable pace. This process cannot—and should not—be rushed. Healing requires patience, allowing us to absorb and integrate each realization with care.

This journey may also bring difficult choices and major shifts. It can be painful to see loved ones set boundaries or seek healing outside the family. Yet as we move forward, change becomes a constant companion. Rather than resisting it, we can learn to embrace this evolution as a

necessary step toward creating a new sense of stability.
For many survivors, fragmented memories and flashbacks create uncertainty and self-doubt. Family members, too, may struggle to reconcile disbelief with the reality of what occurred. But this process is not about proving or disproving the past—it's about recognizing that something happened, something that disrupted the family in undeniable ways.

Our focus is on understanding and addressing the effects, rather than getting lost in debates over details. This approach allows us to move through the aftermath with clarity and purpose. Whether you're a survivor or a family member, acknowledging how sexual harm has influenced your life is an act of courage and self-honesty.

Each person's understanding of the harm they've experienced is their own subjective truth and should not be questioned. How someone interprets and feels an event is deeply personal and cannot be invalidated by another's perspective. By honoring this truth, we create space for healing and clarity to emerge. Over time, as this truth is held without challenge, it often deepens and takes on greater nuance.

There is no single, objective narrative that encompasses everyone's experience. By embracing this multiplicity of perspectives, we free ourselves to explore the impact on our own lives without invalidating anyone else's experiences and how they understand those lived events.

Shifting our focus from "provable objective facts" to the unassailable impact on the individual allows for a more compassionate, inclusive healing process, where each person's journey is honored, even as it intersects with and diverges from others' experiences. This shift is the first step in reclaiming our narrative—not by insisting that others agree with our viewpoint, but by owning our perspective as our own, without the need for validation from others.

Allowing for Anger

Anger plays a strong role in healing from sexual harm, though many of us instinctively shy away from this intense emotion. People often voice concerns such as, "I don't want to feel angry," "I can't access my anger," or "When I express anger, no one listens." The fear that acknowledging anger might harm valued relationships is understandable, but the reality is that anger is an unavoidable part of the healing process. It can take many forms, some healthier than others, but it cannot be ignored or bypassed.

The transformative power of anger lies in its ability to burn up shame. It acts as an alchemical force, transmuting the heavy burden of victimhood into the empowering energy of survivorship. To be clear, this is not advocacy for anger as a permanent state or an invitation to blame and attack others. Anger is the vehicle with which we assert our intrinsic worth as a person who did not deserve what happened to them. Through anger we reclaim our right to exist safely in the world, be treated with basic dignity, have our own agency and set clear boundaries.

When family members respond to sexual harm without anger, it can send an unintended message. A muted or overly analytical approach may suggest that only the survivor feels the injustice of what happened. Without expressed anger from loved ones, the survivor may bear an added burden—the need to convince others of the harm's severity. This shifts the focus from healing to justification, impeding recovery for both the individual and the family.

Anger is not only appropriate but necessary in the face of moral harm. It asserts our humanity when it has been disregarded and signals that we, too, have been impacted. For family members, expressing anger serves multiple purposes: it validates the survivor's experience, affirms that the abuse was profoundly unjust, and acknowledges their own sense of loss.

Sexual harm affects the entire family, and recognizing this truth allows loved ones to claim their own grievance—one that is real and deserving of attention. By doing so, they assert their right to heal alongside the survivor.

When anger is shared rather than suppressed, it becomes a force for connection rather than isolation. It unites the family in acknowledging the harm, ensuring that the survivor does not have to carry the weight alone. In this way, expressing anger is not just a reaction; it is an act of solidarity, a declaration that no one should face this injustice alone or in silence.

Of course, there are potential pitfalls of anger, especially uncontrolled rage. It can destroy relationships and isolate the person expressing it. Many survivors have attempted to share their experiences, only to find their anger met with closing doors. Their attempt to express their truth exacerbated their isolation. However, anger remains a key component to healing from sexual harm. It is possible to build the ability to tap into anger without retraumatizing ourselves and others.

Safe, healing anger expresses the inner world of someone deeply harmed, with all the necessary intensity, but without causing harm to others. It's a controlled burn rather than a wildfire. Expressing anger safely is a skill that requires practice and support. Finding people who can hold space for this level of rage is part of facing harm. The distinction between offensive and defensive anger shows how we can express anger in a way that heals rather than harms, that empowers rather than destroys.

Embracing anger doesn't mean becoming an angry person. It means allowing this potent emotion to play its role in the healing process, burning away shame and helping to forge a stronger, more empowered self. Working through anger is a necessary step for both the survivor and the entire family system as they move through this second phase of healing.

Offensive Anger

Offensive anger is a formidable yet perilous force, often inflicting as much harm on the person wielding it as on its intended target. This form of anger moves beyond holding someone accountable for their actions and instead attacks their character, diminishing their humanity and shifting the focus from the harm itself to the worth of the one who caused it.

Offensive anger manifests as blame, contempt, and criticism, as an attempt to discredit or diminish another. While it may feel justified, even cathartic, it does not lead to healing. Instead, it is a reaction rooted in shame, redirecting attention away from our own pain. Though it may offer a fleeting sense of power, it often deepens disconnection, as the acknowledgment and support we seek are not received.

It is natural to feel overwhelming anger when the harm is profound, and sexual abuse is enough to provoke an outsized emotional response. When that force is coupled with offensive anger, the anger that seeks to strip another of their humanity, it can feel disproportionate to those hearing or witnessing it. This can divide communities into opposing sides—*Team Victim v. Team Offender*—shutting down opportunities for deeper understanding and repair.

When offensive anger escalates into rage, it can re-traumatize the one expressing it, creating further isolation. The recipient may shut down, retaliate, or even garner sympathy from bystanders, leaving the speaker feeling unheard and even more misunderstood. Whenever we attempt to force accountability through dehumanization, we lose our way on the healing path. True accountability is not about punishment or revenge—it is about asking to be seen, heard, and witnessed in the full weight of the harm.

Anger can be a force for justice and healing, but only when it moves us toward connection rather than destruction.

With Whom to Express Our Anger

Anger needs a witness, but not every person is the right one to receive it. Healing does not require confronting the person who caused the harm, nor does it depend on seeking support from family members who may be unwilling or unable to hold space for our experience. The goal is not a binary choice between carrying the weight of shame alone or cutting ties with those we love. A middle path exists—one that allows for healing without the wholesale destruction of relationships.

The fire of anger, powerful enough to burn away shame, can just as easily consume the bridges that connect us to others, leaving us stranded. As we navigate this process, we must choose carefully with whom we share our pain. Some family members may be worth that effort, while others may not yet have the capacity to engage with our experience in a meaningful way. This is not a test of loyalty, nor a measure of who loves us most. It is a recognition that healing requires discernment.

Not everyone is equipped to receive the full force of our anger, and expecting them to do so can create further distance rather than repair. Expressing our pain in spaces where it can be truly heard and held without challenge, allows us to process it without potentially deepening disconnection. Whether that is with a trusted friend, a family ally, a therapist, support group, or in private reflection. Healing is not about forcing others to understand; it is about finding the right places to be witnessed, so we are not left shouting into the void.

Creating a supportive community is an essential part of healing. This group does not need to include our family of origin or even family at all. What matters is identifying those willing to engage in the healing process while setting boundaries with those who repeatedly fall short. At the same time, thoughtful discernment is key. Severing ties may feel like the only option when someone disappoints us, but in many cases, a well-placed boundary can provide the protection we need without unnecessary loss.

To navigate this, we must distinguish between holding others to unrealistic standards and recognizing when a relationship is truly harmful. The difference lies in whether a person's limitations leave us feeling disappointed or whether their actions actively cause harm. If someone struggles to meet our needs but still cares for us in meaningful ways, distance, rather than disconnection,may be the healthiest choice. On the other hand, if their behavior consistently disregards our well-being, it may be necessary to step away entirely. True discernment requires honesty: Are we seeking perfection in others, or are we protecting ourselves from real and ongoing harm?

Some loved ones may never be able to fully acknowledge or validate the impact of sexual harm in our lives. However, that doesn't mean they have no place in our world. We can choose to engage with them in ways that feel safe, placing them at a distance where we are no longer hurt by their limitations while still appreciating what they do offer. Instead of exhausting ourselves trying to change them, we can redirect that energy toward relationships that are truly nourishing.

Humans are complex—more than their mistakes, shortcomings, or single aspects of their identity. While it can be difficult to hold this perspective in the aftermath of abuse, doing so creates more space for healing. Reducing someone solely to their harmful behaviors may feel justified, but it ultimately narrows our ability to move forward. Healing is not about absolving harm but about refusing to be defined by it.

This brings us to the transformative power of **defensive anger**. Unlike offensive anger, which diminishes another's humanity, defensive anger asserts our own. Instead of communicating, "You are a monster for what you did!" defensive anger declares, "I did not deserve what you did to me. I am worth more and am not less-than because of your behavior." The focus shifts inward. This is not to avoid accountability, but to reclaim our dignity and worth.

When we express our truth without attacking, we burn through shame rather than spreading it. Anger, when wielded as a tool for healing rather than a weapon for retaliation, allows us to break cycles of harm rather than repeat them. In the next section, we will explore how to harness defensive anger in a way that affirms both our pain and our worth, while ensuring that in seeking justice, we do not lose ourselves along the way.

Defensive Anger: Sharing To Be Known

Defensive anger is a potent instrument in our healing arsenal. It articulates how specific actions or systemic failures have altered, wounded, and forced unwelcome changes in our lives. This form of anger focuses on the impact of someone's actions or inactions. How those behaviors, words, events changed our inner world or external life, rather than fixating on the qualities of the actor. While these qualities may have contributed to our harm, defensive anger keeps us anchored to our current inner landscape, within our own personal boundaries.

For example, instead of saying, "You are a selfish, cruel person for not protecting me," defensive anger shifts the focus inward: "When you ignored what was happening, I felt abandoned. It left me feeling unprotected and questioning my worth. I needed you to see me and intervene, and when you didn't, it changed how I saw myself and what I believed I deserved." This approach does not excuse the harm, but it ensures that our anger serves our healing rather than pulling us into cycles of blame that leave us unheard and unseen.

In expressing defensive anger, we unveil our reality—our unique perception and experience of the world. This type of anger requires us to speak from the rawness of our pain rather than from a place of attack. Because of this, defensive anger leaves us more vulnerable, which is why offensive anger often feels safer.

Offensive anger says, "You are sick and heartless for what you did," shielding us with blame and indignation. Defensive anger, on the other hand, says, "What you did hurt me deeply. I felt invisible, unworthy, and discarded. I needed you to care, and you didn't." The latter is harder to say because it exposes our wounds rather than protecting us with rage.

For this reason, we must choose wisely when expressing defensive anger, sharing it only with those who have the capacity to hold it with us. Not everyone will be able to sit with our pain, and forcing our vulnerability into unreceptive spaces can deepen our hurt. Understanding when, where, and with whom to share is part of reclaiming our power in the healing process.

Our personal truth is inviolable; only we can truly know the intricacies of our inner realm, our perspective, and the depth of our feelings. These subjective truths, when presented as such, call for acknowledgment and respect. They can not be reasonably challenged. How harm has changed us is something only we know or only something we can find out for ourselves.

Witnessing another's inner world as they express it through defensive anger can be painful. Our natural instinct might be to try to "fix it" or find a way out—both for the speaker and ourselves. We feel bad and suffer with that person. We want it to go away for both of us. However, this impulse, while well-intentioned, can hinder the healing process. The power of defensive anger lies not in our response, but in our ability to simply witness it and sit in discomfort with the speaker.

For example, if someone says, "You missed some obvious signs of abuse, and my life has been forever altered by knowing I wasn't safe. I don't trust people, which impacts my ability to have the relationships I want," we might be tempted to respond defensively with, "Well, how was I supposed to know that was happening? You never told me!" Such a response will undoubtedly make the speaker feel worse.

Alternatively, we might try to fix the situation by saying, "I have been a horrible parent. What can I do now to make it up to you?" That approach may feel burdensome to the speaker, forcing them to determine compensation for harm that has permanently changed their life. The most important response is to listen deeply and acknowledge the speaker's pain. While saying "I'm sorry" is a good response, it only holds genuine meaning if we are feeling the pain we caused when we say it.

When someone shares their experiences, our role is to hold space, to listen deeply without attempting to change their narrative or offer solutions. We aren't required to agree or share their viewpoint. Instead, our task is to hold their pain with compassion and accompany them in their exploration. We accept that this is their inner truth in this moment; we can hold it, but only they can transform it.

The distinction between our reactions to offensive and defensive anger is significant. Offensive anger often carries an underlying message such as, "You are less worthy as a human being," which naturally provokes defensiveness.

For example, imagine an adult who was harmed by their mother describing her as a "monster" who is evil and should be thrown in jail to prevent her from hurting future generations. A sibling hearing this might compare that harsh portrayal with their own, more nuanced experiences of their mother and feel compelled to retreat rather than accept an oversimplified, dehumanizing view. This example shows how, whether we know someone personally or not, we instinctively resist offensive anger by defending the full humanity of the person being attacked, often leaving the speaker feeling unseen.

Defensive anger, conversely, carries a different underlying message: "I deserved more. I am worth more than how I was treated. Can you be with me while I explore and express it?" While this kind of anger can also be challenging to hold, it's not because it pushes us away, but because it invites us into an often emotionally intense intimacy with another.

This kind of anger, rooted in vulnerability, is more likely to evoke compassion from the listener. And that is what the speaker is seeking and ultimately needs. In these moments, there's no pressure to fix or explain. What matters most is simply being present: to witness without judgment as the speaker gives voice to their inner world and begins to discover their own path forward.

Cultivating the skill to express anger constructively allows us to share our pain while maintaining important relationships. When expressed with intention, anger can help release us from the blame that often accompanies abuse. It awakens our sense of power, enabling us to acknowledge the wrongness of the situation. Transformation occurs when we recognize and assert that the shame caused by the abuse does not belong to us.

The Green Path is not linear; rather, it unfolds in unpredictable patterns, marked by alternating moments of progress and pause. It calls for resolve, endurance, and—above all—kindness toward ourselves and those facing similar challenges. As we proceed, let's remember that our experiences, anger, and healing are uniquely our own. By sharing these truths, we forge bonds that support us during our most difficult moments.

Next, let's consider how offensive and defensive expressions of anger might manifest in a real-life situation. Imagine a scenario involving a mother and daughter, where the daughter discloses that she was sexually abused by the mother's massage therapist or healer. We will examine two variations of this disclosure: one characterized by offensive anger and the other by defensive anger.

A Mother/Daughter Story

Patricia, in her forties with children and a successful career and children of her own, grappled with depression. During therapy, memories of childhood abuse by her mother's "healer" resurfaced. Determined to confront this past, Patricia approached her mother.

First Conversation (Offensive Anger)

> **Patricia:** "Mom. I want to tell you something. When I was so young, you brought me to your so called *spiritual healer*, that creepy massage therapist who anyone could see was not a healer, and he sexually abused me. Did you know!? How could you not have known? Was sex a part of your sessions with him too? I was 8 years old! How could you have done that to me? Were you somehow getting off on that? Was he paying you? My life is ruined

and for what? You are not just a horrible parent, you are basically a perpetrator yourself!"

Mother: "That is ridiculous! You are making that up. He was a deeply spiritual man who saved my life routinely. Just because you are now a big shot at work and your husband convinced you to stop believing in alternative healing, doesn't mean he wasn't helping you too. You probably owe your success to his sessions. Why do you have to attack everything I do, as if I am the cause of all your self-absorbed depression? I have devoted my whole life to your care and this is the thanks I get? You are nothing but spoiled and delusional, always looking for someone else to blame for your misery."

Offensive Anger Approach:

This exchange, while painful, is not an atypical interaction between a mother and daughter when such devastating harm initially comes to light. These are incredibly difficult conversations, laden with raw emotion and years of unprocessed trauma. While they can do damage, it is not easy to navigate a conversation when offensive anger is present.

For Patricia, confronting the parent who was supposed to ensure her safety is an act of courage. For her mother, being suddenly faced with the possibility that she unknowingly exposed her child to harm is nothing short of devastating. Our natural instinct when we're hurt and angry is often to blame, and when we're blamed, we instinctively defend ourselves. This dynamic, while understandable, often leads to another wave of harm.

These initial reactions don't define either person. The mother's defensiveness doesn't reflect her full range of feelings about this situation, just as Patricia's accusatory tone doesn't encompass the full complexity of her feelings about her mother. For the mother, incorporating this information into her own history with the therapist who she remembers as helpful is an enormous psychological task that can't be accomplished in a single moment.

These conversations are a starting point, not an endpoint. They reveal the need for healing on both sides and underscore the importance of learning to express anger in ways that open doors rather than close them. As we move forward, we'll explore how to navigate these challenging waters with more skill and compassion.

Second Conversation (Defensive Anger)

Patricia: "Mom, I want to talk to you about something that is going to be hard to hear. Are you OK with having this conversation with me right now?"

Mother: "You are scaring me. I definitely want to hear anything you have to tell me but let me sit down first. Let's go on the porch."

Patricia: "Remember that massage therapist, the healer you used to go to?"

Mother: ""Of course. (dread starting to rise) I used to take you for treatments in his office."

Patricia: "Right. And he used to touch me inappropriately, and tell me not to tell you because you would be angry. So I didn't. He told me I would be punished for not doing what he said. His abuse progressively got much worse over time. I remember in sixth grade making myself sick so I wouldn't have to go. I believe my lifelong depression stems from these experiences. This abuse has ruined so much of my life. The injustice of it. It is so unfair, disgusting and wrong!" her voice rising with every word.

Mother: (crying now, burying her face)

Patricia: (still with raised voice) "I am really suffering from this, mom. This has impacted every aspect of my life. I have never understood why I can't stand to go to the doctor. How I can't sleep easily at night. My marriage is struggling because I have such a hard time with sex. I just want to stay at work, and not come home. It just isn't fair what I have had to go through in my life because of this man and what he did. I was getting so depressed earlier this year. I wanted to leave the world - though I could never do that to my kids. I am just so angry about everything I go through because of this criminal act." She stops, takes a deep breath, sits back relaxing her muscles and closes her eyes.

Mother: (visibly shaken) "I am stunned. I...I am so sorry. I can barely wrap my mind around what you are telling me. Thank you for telling me. What can I do?"

Defensive Anger Approach:

The second conversation illustrates defensive anger. The daughter's anger is strong, but it's expressed by describing how the situation has affected her life rather than accusing her mother or focusing on the offender's character. This change in approach creates space for both parties to navigate the difficult moment with greater openness.

The daughter can begin to fully express her pain and anger, while the mother has space to absorb the shocking information without triggering a reflex to defend herself. This approach creates room for a more compassionate and productive dialogue, potentially serving as a foundation for boundaried understanding within the family system in future conversations.

These are the skills we need to walk *The Green Path*. We take the necessary time to explore the unique impact of the shame events on ourselves, express them with others who will witness them without judgment. While The Green Path may begin in the shadow of harm, it leads us towards light, toward reclaiming our power, establishing healthier boundaries, and forging deeper, more authentic connections. Every step, no matter how small, is a victory in our healing journey.

CHAPTER 12

The Purple Path: Healing from Causing Harm

The Purple Path is a journey of accountability and repair for anyone who has caused harm—whether through direct actions, inaction, or harmful responses. It's not only for those who committed sexual harm, but also for those whose reactions in the aftermath deepened the wound, silenced the truth, or fractured trust when it was most needed.

Intersecting traumas, misguided coping mechanisms, and even small, hurtful behaviors all exist on the same continuum. The difficulty of the journey varies, but the fundamental steps remain the same: recognizing the harm, taking responsibility, and making meaningful repair when possible.

No one teaches us how to walk this path. Families are often left to navigate harm without guidance, and in the absence of a clear framework, they may respond in ways that cause further damage, sometimes unintentionally, sometimes in an effort to regain control or protect what feels familiar.

Accountability is not about punishment or self-condemnation. It is about honesty, courage, and the willingness to own our impact, no matter how uncomfortable. When done with care, this work has the power to repair relationships, restore trust, and shift long-standing family patterns.

This path applies not only to those who have caused the initial harm but also to family members whose words and actions—whether reactive, avoidant, or defensive—have intensified the pain of others. Some examples include:

A non-offending parent who struggles to acknowledge the harm without pointing out the happy times the family has had in the past..

A sibling of both the victim and offender who justifies staying connected to the offender by blaming the survivor for unrelated issues.

A partner of a survivor who discloses the abuse to family members without the survivor's consent, deepening their sense of lost control.

A partner of someone who caused harm who insists they should be included in family gatherings by shifting blame onto others.

A survivor who, after multiple family-sponsored treatment programs, continues to demand support while not acknowledging the strain on the family resources.

A person who caused harm as a minor who struggles with accountability, qualifying their remorse by pointing out their own past victimization.

Each of these examples illustrates how harm does not end with a single event. It continues outward, often compounding pain as it sets off more reactions in others. However, the path forward remains the same. We stop when we become aware and remorseful for the harm we have caused to others, and take responsibility.

This is true even when the harm caused to us is greater than the harm we have inflicted on another by all reasonable standards. The Purple Path is not about erasing the past; it is about changing the future. As we engage in our "purple work" we will make it safer for others to do so too. We will set the momentum going in a different direction, inspiring others to feel they too can walk the Purple Path.

The Purple Path invites us to embrace a challenging truth: restoring a family system after child sexual abuse—or any significant harm—requires taking responsibility for our role in the dysfunction. It's tempting to reduce the narrative of harm to a single victim and a single offender, casting everyone else as bystanders. Similarly, we may create a hierarchy of suffering, focusing solely on the person who endured the most while dismissing others as not having experienced enough to deserve attention.

Harm within a family rarely exists in isolation. The offender may be deceased, unwilling to engage, or entirely absent from the family, yet the effects linger. This path is for all of us who may not have been our best selves within the family system at times to reflect and take responsibility. Honest self-examination often reveals ways, however small, in which we may have perpetuated harm or failed to act when needed.

Healing is not just an individual pursuit but a collective process. If everyone claims only a form of victimhood or innocent bystander and no one accepts any level of responsibility, the path forward becomes obstructed. By examining our own actions and inactions, we begin to clear those obstacles and model accountability for others.

The responsibility borne by the person who caused sexual harm is of a different magnitude than that of family members whose actions or inactions allowed harm to occur, remain unaddressed, or persist in some form of denial. Each role in the system, however, deserves honest examination and accountability.

By expanding the understanding of harm to include the entire family system, accountability becomes a shared responsibility rather than an individual burden. This shift moves the focus away from blame, which isolates and fractures relationships, and toward collective recognition of the ways dysfunction has shaped family dynamics. When the family as a whole takes responsibility for its patterns and responses, both the breakdown and the repair become clearer, more realistic, and more achievable.

This is not a path of blame or unending guilt, nor is it about proving anyone's innocence or wrongdoing. Instead, it is an opportunity for honest reflection, shared accountability, and a commitment to strengthening the family system. It challenges family members to listen deeply to the effects of their choices, not just as individuals, but as part of an interconnected whole. By acknowledging how harm reverberates through the family, they can take appropriate responsibility, make space for repair, and work together to rebuild trust and connection.

Trust can be rebuilt through genuine accountability and a demonstrated commitment to trustworthiness. Though there may be reasons why harm occurred, we must focus on individual impact, and address the systemic failures that allow harm to continue through the ways in which we are relating.

A family system has immense potential—either to perpetuate dysfunction or to nurture restoration. By engaging intentionally with its dynamics, we unlock the possibility of a more complete recovery, one that prevents further harm and creates a foundation of safety and connection for everyone involved.

The Purple Path is founded on two essential practices: 1 - Recognizing the impact of our behavior through empathic listening and 2 - Feeling genuine remorse. These interconnected steps form the bedrock for taking responsibility and actively participating in the healing process.

Empathic Listening: Listening to Know

The Purple Path begins with empathic listening, a practice that requires us to set aside our personal defenses and narratives to fully absorb the pain we've caused others. It's about holding space for the hurt we've inflicted and letting it be expressed.

When someone we've harmed shares their pain, they're offering us a precious gift; a chance to repair and heal together. Many who have experienced life-altering harm choose to walk away, having no desire to communicate with those who hurt them. This is an understandable response that we must respect. In such cases, refrain from approaching the person who was harmed.

If we initiate a chance for repair, especially if they were not expecting us to, it may occur to them as prioritizing our needs over theirs. It may also cause them to once again feel out of control and retraumatized by our raising the subject when they were not ready or in a safe place to have that conversation.

If someone we've harmed confronts us, acknowledge the courage and trust it takes for them to do so. This moment is a rare opportunity to hear how our actions have affected them and to take responsibility. By listening without defensiveness, we might be able to create a safe space for them to share their personal truth openly. This act of witnessing can have a deeper impact than anything we might say in response.

Empathic listening means listening to comprehend the inner world of the other. This requires attentive silence. Our job is to listen, not explain ourselves. We give the person our complete attention, allowing them to express their experience freely without interruption. We focus on what they have been through, not what we have been through.

This may feel like punishment, but it is not. It is an invitation to participate in the healing process. While it's important to maintain our sense of worth, expressing our inherent goodness during an opportunity for empathic listening can be counterproductive. Instead, connect with our humanity as we step into deep listening. The stronger our sense of worth, the more steadily we can listen when confronted with the negative impact of our actions.

If we are not ready to hold space with empathy, it is better to ask for more time to do our internal work rather than risk causing harm. Rushing into the conversation unprepared may lead us to shift the focus onto ourselves or how we are feeling, undermining the opportunity for genuine witnessing and supporting the other.

It is more respectful to acknowledge that the situation calls for empathy and understanding, even if we are not currently able to provide it. If hearing about how we've harmed someone triggers a shame spiral, it's also wise to pause the conversation until we can approach it with a calm and grounded mindset.

Healing is not something that happens in a single conversation. It's a gradual process that unfolds whenever we create enough safety to truly listen to someone's experience and respond thoughtfully, meeting their needs where we can. It requires a strong sense of worth to take responsibility for the impact of our behavior without succumbing to a sense that we are a horrible person.

We must care for our own well-being in order to show up fully for these conversations. When we don't have the bandwidth to engage thoughtfully, it's okay to acknowledge that and offer to return to the conversation when we are able. Healing is a marathon, not a sprint, and every step forward counts.

Genuine Remorse

Remorse and guilt may look similar, but they come from very different places. Most of us apologize out of guilt—often driven by fear. We fear being judged, facing consequences, or being seen as someone we are not. We worry about being misunderstood or labeled in ways that feel impossible to undo.

Whether the harm is small, like forgetting a birthday, or profound, like sexual abuse, the person receiving the apology can usually tell when it's more about easing our own discomfort than addressing their pain.

If our goal is to relieve guilt, avoid consequences, or protect ourselves, the apology will feel hollow. And if we, as family members, support apologies rooted in guilt, we risk being seen as complicit. These apologies lack the authenticity needed to repair relationships and often deepen the disconnection.

Genuine Remorse is something else entirely. It requires strength and humility to set aside fear and fully face the pain we've caused. True remorse means we not only understand the harm intellectually, but feel its weight in our bodies and hearts. It's the willingness to stay present with another's suffering—not just to say "I'm sorry," but to truly absorb the impact of our actions.

This takes time and inner work. Feeling another's pain without turning away is not easy. Without this emotional awareness, apologies remain performative. They serve only to ease our own conscience or appear to others like we are trying, rather than offering meaningful repair.

A common frustration for those trying to make amends for significant harm to a loved one is the sense that their apologies are ignored or rejected. *"How many times do I have to say I'm sorry?"* often signals we've lost sight of what truly matters. The goal is not to have our apology accepted, but to keep doing the work: to listen, to understand, to empathize and to allow trust to rebuild over time. Repair is not a single conversation; it's a sustained commitment.

When opportunities arise to listen to those we've harmed and value the relationship enough to make the effort, we take them. Healing happens in small, meaningful moments. The person we hurt may not be able or willing to engage directly. Still, there are often others in the family system or community who have also been impacted and may be open to connection.

Repair is not something we schedule or control. It unfolds when the moment allows, with the people who allow it. It might be in a quiet exchange, a family gathering, or an unexpected conversation. What matters is our willingness to show up with presence and humility when those doors open, however briefly.

These moments may seem small or fleeting, but when met with real awareness that comes from internal work, they can shift something. A comment left unchallenged, a memory named without defensiveness, a pause long enough to feel and therefore acknowledge another's pain. Each is a step on the path of repair. No single act will make things whole, but taken together, they create a rhythm of integrity that others can come to trust.

This is not about becoming a punching bag. Our humanity must remain intact. To do this work well, we have to stay connected to our own worth even as we acknowledge the harm we've caused. Remorse is not submission. It is strength rooted in compassion. We stay grounded, and when pain surfaces, we meet it with openness, not avoidance. We disengage when we are losing our footing, and get the support and self care we need to try again later.

This is not a call to live in a constant state of self-punishment. Most days, we live our lives as best we can: working, connecting, growing, evolving. And, when a moment comes that calls us to bear witness, to offer help, to feel the pain our past actions have caused, we answer that call with care. These moments do not define the entirety of who we are, but they do shape who we are becoming.

The Purple Path is a commitment to meet those moments with genuine remorse and courage. It is the willingness to show up with honesty and heart, whether the person we harmed is ready to engage or not. We extend that same care to others who may be feeling affected at that moment. This path doesn't require perfection, only presence, a sustained practice of accountability, rooted in love.

We can choose to be bystanders, watching from the sidelines, or upstanders, actively engaging as a full member of the system. While it is widely understood that child sexual abuse can create a shame event capable of derailing a victim's life, the focus cannot be on our apology.

What truly matters is creating space for the one harmed to express the impact of their experience if they want to, and with some basic boundaries. Allowing them to share their story in their own words, with as much emotion as they need, and being present enough to feel it with them is what begins to heal the damage.

This healing does not happen all at once but unfolds in small, meaningful increments over time.These opportunities are rare and take time to unfold. We may not have access to the person we harmed directly, but in all likelihood, there are others in our family who have been impacted indirectly. We can begin with the doors that are open to us.

Accountability is not a one-time event but an ongoing process—one that requires the courage to face shame, compassion for the pain we've caused, and a sustained commitment to repair relationships wherever possible. This work lays the foundation for healing, not just for ourselves but for those we've hurt and the broader family system.

We may not see the results we hope for right away, or perhaps never. Yet, the Purple Path calls us to face the pain we've caused directly, embracing a journey of accountability and transformation regardless of the outcome. By confronting harm with honesty and genuine remorse, we take the first steps toward mending what was broken. This is a path to becoming better versions of ourselves while fostering healing in ways we may never fully see or understand.

***A Purple Story:** The Wedding*

Steven approached his cousin's wedding with a mix of excitement and apprehension. While close to this cousin, family gatherings had become a source of stress since he confronted his older brother, Joe, about the sexual abuse that occurred when Steven was 9 and Joe was 12.

Steven felt proud of breaking the silence, and appreciated Joe's acknowledgement even if Joe downplayed it as childhood rough housing. Steven had stood his ground, reminding Joe of the secrecy he had imposed by telling him if he told their mom, they would both be in trouble. Joe acknowledged it, felt a wave of shame, and the conversation ended there.

Entering the wedding venue, Steven was struck by the sight of his family sitting together, enjoying one another. Kids on their laps, laughing and happy. He felt a wave of anger that turned into grief. After disclosing to them, and confronting his brother last year, Steven took some distance to get himself steady and feel some new boundaries. His parents understood.

Now, looking at all of them it seems they haven't thought about him at all. Life just continued on as it had before, as if nothing had happened. The contrast with his own emotional turmoil was jarring. As he sat down next to them, the group got suddenly quiet and nervous. It spoke volumes.

After the wedding, Steven called his mother, expressing his hurt at the family's behavior. He started out saying, "Mom. I feel really hurt by the way you all treated me at the wedding. What the hell? I am the one who was victimized but somehow Joe is still the center of everyone's attention and I am the odd man out."

His mother's response, while well-intentioned, was based in guilt and self interest:

"I'm so sorry, Steven, but you have to understand. Those are my only grandchildren, and they need me. I can't walk away from your brother and his family. He's my son. I'm sorry for what you went through, but what do you want me to do about it now? It breaks my

heart, it truly does.

Your brother felt awful after you told us last year. His wife said he was in bed for days. I think that's punishment enough, don't you? We don't want to break up the whole family because of this, do we?"

While we can understand the mother's struggle to balance family relationships, her response likely left Steven feeling diminished and sidelined for the sake of family unity. Her apology, rooted in guilt, prioritized explaining her actions over listening to Steven's pain.

While we can understand the mother's struggle to balance family relationships, her response likely left Steven feeling diminished and sidelined for the sake of family unity. Her apology, rooted in guilt, prioritized explaining her actions over listening to Steven's pain.

After that conversation with his mother, Steven's brother reached out. He asked if Steven would meet him for coffee. Steven agreed. When they sat down, his brother began by saying "I want to fix this." He started to explain how other boys were doing something similar to him at the time. That he had only been reacting to the environment around him. He blamed their parents for not keeping them both safe. Steven stood up and walked out without a word. Another year passed before they saw each other again, and the distance between them had only grown.

This exchange with his mother may not have offered Steven immediate comfort. Her words—"*I didn't know how to talk about it*"—may still have landed as a painful reminder of how she had failed to imagine what he had been carrying over the past year. If, instead, she had offered him an opportunity to speak without defending herself or minimizing his pain, she would have signaled a shift. Not a request for forgiveness, but a desire to witness the reality of his experience.

There is quiet power in simply being present. A statement like, "*I know I've been focused on how hard this was for me, and I haven't thought about or asked how it's been for you. I'm sorry about that, and if you're willing, I want to listen now,*" could have acknowledged the gap between them and offered a bridge. Even if Steven couldn't accept her invitation at that moment, it might have opened a door.

When Steven's brother reached out to meet for coffee, things might have gone differently too. Instead of explaining or justifying his actions, he could have started with, "*I know I caused you harm, and I've been afraid to face it. I want to understand what that was like for you. I'm not here to defend myself. I'm here to listen.*" That single act of humility, the willingness to set aside his own fear and center Steven's experience, could have made space for something real to begin.

Even if his intention was to repair the relationship, it would have been more powerful had he resisted the urge to frame it as a problem to solve or push for resolution in a first conversation. Instead of saying, "*I want to fix this,*" he could have allowed the long, often uncertain process of healing to unfold on Steven's terms. True repair doesn't begin with answers. It begins with a willingness to be present to what is, by taking responsibility regardless of circumstances, and staying in the discomfort of not knowing or being able to control the outcome.

Most of us don't get it right at first. We understandably miss what's needed. No one teaches us how to heal from having caused significant harm to another, beyond some basic idea of apologizing. When that doesn't work, we choose silence or other forms of self-protection, as humans do. Maya Angelou reminds us, when we know better, we can do better. These small moments of listening, feeling and understanding become the building blocks of trust, and the slow return of connection. They make it possible, over time, for someone like Steven to feel safe enough to step back into the family—not by obligation, but by choice.

CHAPTER 13

Releasing the Shame Event: It Finds You

As we reach this phase on the path to healing from harm, we begin to experience the gradual process of releasing. The emotional intensity of the shame event has faded in some ways. This isn't a deliberate action but a natural outcome of the internal work we have done in facing the harm. It is not a final destination but a gentle shift in how we relate to both our past and present. We find we are standing on more solid ground.

This phase unfolds subtly. We might notice one day that the heaviness feels a bit lighter, our steps a little steadier. Perhaps a laugh escapes us without restraint, or we face a difficult moment with resilience we had not had in the past. These moments, though small, mark the progress of healing, a quiet, steady integration of the work we've done.

Healing isn't a straight line. We will still face plenty of challenges and return to old coping mechanisms. There will be many more painful moments when we must face the harm event. The transitions go back and forth but become easier over time. We are more familiar with how these waves come and how they go. Brief stretches of lightness—several good days strung together—signal that we are learning to trust the process. Each step forward, even if followed by a step back, is progress.

As this shift happens, we might begin to notice changes in our external lives as well. A kind word from a colleague, a new friendship, or an evening spent reading instead of numbing ourselves are all signs of the healing that has been happening beneath the surface. Like a wound quietly closing, these changes often go unnoticed.

Self-compassion deepens during this time, allowing us to approach our mistakes and those of others with more grace and understanding. This kindness toward ourselves often extends outward, softening our judgments of others and strengthening our connections. We are more accepting of the complexity of human experiences and relationships, which results in feeling less alone.

Gradually, our sense of worth grows. We set boundaries more confidently, express our needs more clearly, and release others from unrealistic expectations. We let go of fantasies about who will or will not support us, focusing instead on what is real and present. Healing comes with the recognition that while support is valuable, our journey is ultimately our responsibility.

For those healing from being harmed, it is not about forgiveness. In fact, forgiveness has very little to do with this third phase. We know we are healing when our long term symptoms are less potent. When we see ourselves reclaiming our lives as our own, and feeling joy. When we no longer see the shame event as a major defining aspect of our identity. It is part of our story, but not the most important part.

For those who are healing from having caused harm, we know we are healing when we have the capacity to make a genuine apology. We may not have the opportunity but if given a chance to show our remorse, we have done the work to find it. Our commitment to making the world a better place and being sensitive to the impact we have on others is a good sign of our healing. Not as a punishment but as our lifelong responsibility we accept graciously.

When long-term symptoms of harm begin to fade, we are left with more internal space for new experiences. We might feel safer, more trusting, and more discerning about where we spend our energy. This allows us to navigate relationships intentionally, maintaining our boundaries and honoring the boundaries of others. We start to let go of the need to carry others who are not ready to heal.

In this phase, joy starts to re-enter our lives. We allow ourselves to feel happiness without guilt, recognizing that embracing joy does not diminish our past or the work we have done or the future work we will do to heal. We make choices aligned with our well-being, closing doors on situations that no longer serve us and opening new ones with confidence.

Releasing trauma is not about forgetting or "getting over" our experiences; it's about weaving them into our life story in a way that lets us move forward with authenticity. Healing unfolds in cycles, as new layers of our experience come to light. When we notice moments of compassion for ourselves and others, we know we are healing. This compassion cannot be forced, but it can find us when we are open to it.

Healing is an ongoing journey, not a destination. As we release and integrate, we honor the path we've traveled while remaining open to continued growth. In this space of release, we discover a quiet calm, a reminder, even if fleeting, that we are going to be okay.

The world is starting to soften.

PART IV

CHAPTER 14

Healing Together Starts Apart

Not everyone in a family is the victim of sexual harm, but everyone has been traumatized by the abuse and its aftermath.

For survivors, witnessing family members grappling with the effects of the trauma can lessen their sense of isolation. Recognizing that others feel the weight of what has occurred fosters a shared understanding. I once heard a victim say to their non-offending parent "what about how this has damaged your life? Why are you always talking about how it damaged mine?"

When sexual harm disrupts a family, the instinct is often to focus all attention on the person who was harmed. To offer them support, try to fix it, or encourage them to move forward. That's only a small part of what's needed. The deeper work begins when each family member starts to examine how the harm affected their own life.

Sexual harm doesn't just impact one person. When loved ones

acknowledge their own pain, anger, guilt, and betrayal they are demonstrating the true nature of this violation. When we see our own fractured relationships, or feelings of powerlessness, then we begin to engage ourselves in what the family needs. This is what creates the conditions for collective repair.

And something important happens when the person who was harmed sees that others are affected too—not in ways that overshadow their pain, but in ways that reflect it. There can be relief in knowing they're not the only one carrying the weight. That others are hurting too. That they are not alone.

If you've ever wondered why a survivor "can't get over it," the harder truth may be this: they may still be surrounded by people who haven't started their own work. And so they're left navigating not just their own pain, but the unspoken, unprocessed pain of everyone around them.

So who is actually struggling to "get over it"? The survivor who has been in therapy for years? Or the family members who have not yet taken any steps to identify the impact on their own lives?

Ignoring the harm, avoiding the topic, or waiting for someone else to change isn't doing the internal work. And if it feels like all the energy is centered on the survivor, it may be because they have also bought into the mistaken idea that their healing is the key to everyone else's peace. That's a heavy, lonely burden. And it doesn't work that way.

Real change happens when every member of the family takes responsibility for the ways they've been impacted and the ways they've responded. This isn't about blame. It's about stepping into the reflective nature of how we heal, a process that belongs to each of us.

The Challenge of Expectations

We set ourselves off in the wrong direction when we focus on someone else's actions as the path to our own stability. When families place the burden of healing on the survivor, they often end up blaming them for the family's fractured state and ongoing discord. Likewise, when survivors tie their healing to the hope that others will acknowledge, change, or behave a certain way, they risk staying stuck and finding themselves isolated.

When both the survivor and their loved ones buy into the idea that someone else can make it better, abdicating their part in the process, things tend to unravel. The pressure builds, and the harm deepens. It can start to feel like a trap no one can escape.

When we cling to what we believe a loving parent, sibling, child, or partner should do, we give away our power. And when those expectations aren't met, as they often are not, we stack fresh pain on top of old wounds. Eventually, we stop responding to what's actually happening and start reacting to what we imagined others should have done. That confusion leads to even more disconnection.

The survivor might say, "What kind of mother sits at a wedding table with the uncle who abused their child?" The pain behind that question is real. But instead of staying stuck in outrage or betrayal, we can shift our focus: *What boundary do I need here to feel safer? What did I expect from my mother in this situation, and was that realistic? What is this showing me about what I can and can't count on from her?*

The longer we wait for someone else to change, the more resentment builds. Families wait for survivors to "move on." Survivors wait for their families to finally see, finally act in the ways they want. Expectations harden into judgment, judgment turns into blame, and blame quietly erodes trust. In the end, no one moves because they do not know how. Individuals give up when they start to feel hopeless that things will ever get better.

Expectations are a labyrinth with no exit. They distract us from the only thing we truly control: our own internal work.

This doesn't mean excusing harmful behavior. People will disappoint us, especially when they haven't done their own work. However, we do not need to measure our well-being by their actions. Other people's choices are data points—not verdicts. Not everyone will recognize the needs of others. Some won't be ready. Some never will. Our job is to keep doing the work that belongs to us.

Letting go of expectations is not giving up. It is claiming authority over our own healing. When we stop trying to manage others and take responsibility for ourselves, we rise out of the maddening labyrinth. We begin to set boundaries without rage, express needs without expectation, and respond to hurt without collapsing into it. The only person who can change in a way that makes us more whole is ourselves.

The Hard Work of Change

Healing often feels worse before it feels better. The upheaval and intensity of emotions can be daunting. There can be expanded resistance in ourselves or others, and that too is often a sign of meaningful growth. Trusting this process and learning to self-soothe during difficult moments is key. Over time, the pain begins to give way to a new sense of self and greater emotional stability.

When even two people in a system commit to their own healing, the entire family culture can begin to shift. These changes take time and may not always be visible immediately, but they set the stage for a new narrative. Repairing a family starts with the only place we have control—ourselves. Through our personal growth, we plant the seeds for collective healing and transformation, offering a chance for the family to evolve into something stronger and more connected than before.

One of the most overlooked challenges we have when we are in pain, is the unrealistic expectation that others should know how to respond to us. The truth is, the people around us are often carrying their own confusion, blame and guilt from the sexual harm and its aftermath. Their reactions, whether withdrawn, defensive, self-centered or emotionally volatile, may reflect wounds we will never fully understand.

This does not mean we must stand and take it, but when we can remind ourselves that we are not the only ones affected it can let in some compassion, and perhaps more importantly a realism of what we can expect. Everyone in the system is navigating intense, often hidden, emotional terrain. Expecting each other to remain grounded and available at all times sets us up for disappointment.

Instead of relying on others to stay regulated at the times we need them to, we can learn to recognize when reactivity or fear is at play, and adjust our expectations and establish our boundaries. When we understand the difference between what we will call the Protective Mind and the Expansive Mind, we gain a powerful tool. Not just for understanding ourselves, but for choosing how we want to show up, especially when others cannot.

Understanding the Protective Mind

The *Protective Mind* is an essential part of being human. It shows up when we sense danger, whether physical, emotional, or relational, and works hard to keep us safe. We don't choose when it turns on. It's automatic, often outside of our conscious control. What we can do is learn to recognize when we or someone else is in that state, and make choices that help restore a sense of safety.

In the *Protective Mind*, our attention narrows. Our own needs take precedence. We may become less aware of others and more focused on managing our discomfort. This isn't selfishness but rather a reflective built-in self-absorption. It keeps us secure but often creates tension in families, especially when everyone is hurting and doesn't have the capacity to fully show up for others.

Each of us carries a personal archive of difficult moments. Some we remember clearly, others are long buried. Over time, our triggers often become less connected to the original harm and more tied to symbolic reminders. A person who once survived a serious car accident may initially feel nervous riding in a fast car. Years later, that same person might feel panicked simply hearing tires screech in the street. The body remembers, even when the mind no longer makes the connection.

This dynamic is especially important to understand in families affected by sexual harm. The topic alone can trigger unconscious reactions. What we often refer to as the "ick factor" around child sexual abuse can lead people to shut down or avoid the conversation entirely. This discomfort sometimes results in what's known as moral dumbfounding—when the *Protective Mind* generates a quick judgment, delivers a firm pronouncement, and refuses further discussion. The Protective Mind isn't interested in new information or alternate perspectives; it seeks only what confirms a fast return to psychological safety.

These reactions can seem disproportionate or illogical until we recognize them as the Protective Mind doing its job, not a reflection of the person's full self or values. These responses are often rooted not in the present moment, but in the listener's own unresolved history. When someone withdraws or becomes reactive, it's not necessarily a rejection. It may simply be their *Protective Mind* trying to move them away from perceived danger.

And here's the challenge: you can't talk someone out of their *Protective Mind*. Logic doesn't land when a person feels unsafe. What helps instead is time, space, movement, water, and gentleness; all conditions that allow the nervous system to settle. Naming what's happening can help too: "This feels overwhelming right now. Let's talk about it later."

In families, we often expect others to respond the way we would or in the way we need or in a way we can at least manage. When they don't, it can feel like betrayal. Most of us, when activated, are doing the best we can to stay afloat. Thinking in terms of the Protective Mind can help us see those moments with more compassion. We can keep ourselves more grounded when we recognize we are all managing pain we don't always fully understand.

Of course, the *Protective Mind* isn't the whole story. There is another part of us—what we call the Expansive Mind—that can engage with openness, creativity, and connection. Learning to recognize which mind is leading in any given moment gives us more choice, more clarity, and more possibility in how we relate to ourselves and each other.

The Expansive Mind

When we feel safe, seen, accepted, and understood, our Expanded Mind is more accessible, and the world takes on a remarkably different hue. In this state, we have the capacity to balance our own interests with genuine care and concern for the interests of others. A sense of abundance emerges, where we feel there is enough to go around. The constant vigilance and need to protect ourselves temporarily fade, allowing us to relax.

Our self-absorption diminishes without losing our sense of self. Feeling understood, we become more open to understanding the experiences of others with curiosity. We stop clinging to black-and-white narratives and begin to make space for differing perspectives without feeling the need to challenge them. From this vantage point, we recognize the countless influences shaping every individual's complex life, fostering compassion for misunderstandings, bad days, and the inevitable growth edges we all face.

In our Expansive Mind, our authenticity shines through. Our personality emerges without fear, and we become less judgmental of ourselves and others. This steadiness produces a contagious sense of hope and possibility. It feels like despite our struggles we will all be okay, which, in turn, makes it more likely that we will be. We naturally override negativity with a more open view, seeing the light and allowing for mistakes in ourselves and others.

Importantly, when we operate from this mindset, it can inspire those around us to access their own Expansive Minds. This generosity of spirit has an influence on the quality of interactions. When we approach others with a calm, inclusive perspective, we offer others a chance to step out of their reactive state and see the situation differently. Imagine someone panicking about missing a flight. If their partner responds calmly, saying, "If we miss it, we miss it. There will be another flight, and we can enjoy a nice dinner at the airport," this grounded response can have a soothing effect on everyone's stress.

Or consider a partner nervous about attending a party where they might see the cousin who harmed them. Responding with reassurance, such as, "You are safe. I'll stay home with you if you'd like, or I'll stay by your side the whole party. You are loved and supported. You have control over this situation, and I am here," empowers them to make the best choice for themselves. This reminder of their agency as an adult and the support they have can help shift their perspective, easing them out of survival mode and into a place of clarity and confidence.

Managing Our Interactions

Healing together requires a foundation of relative safety. When judgment and blame are unleashed, they push everyone into a defensive, survival-focused mindset, making hope and connection harder to sustain. Our inner work involves recognizing when we fall into this self-protective stance and, when possible, learning to climb out of it. When it isn't possible, we acknowledge it as a temporary state and take responsibility for its impact on others once we are ready.

As we commit to addressing harm and its complexities, we acknowledge the important role our fight-or-flight response plays in protecting us. This instinct doesn't vanish, nor should it. Our capacity to sense danger, whether real or perceived, remains a key part of our survival. However, for those who have experienced significant trauma, this response can become heightened, causing us to default to the Protective Mind more quickly and frequently.

At the same time, healing invites us to cultivate an expanding perspective and more inclusive ways of connecting with others.
We prioritize creating environments where we feel safe, seen, and understood, giving ourselves opportunities to practice engaging from a

grounded, Expanded Mind. Recognizing that this isn't always possible in unsafe spaces, we work to establish healthy boundaries and give ourselves permission to say no when needed.

Repairing the family dynamics doesn't come from a single apology, a breakthrough conversation, or a shared decision to move on. It comes from recognizing when we are in our Protective Mind, learning how to limit the damage it can do, and building the capacity to return to a more neutral state; steadily, and with intention. The more we commit to keeping strong boundaries, allowing or asking others to do the same, the more often we can remain in that neutral zone, where clarity and choice are possible.

We don't get rid of the Protective Mind. We learn how to work with it. And when we can access our Expansive Mind, even briefly, we offer something meaningful to the people around us: a different way of being in the world that vibrates in a higher realm. Healing, in this context, becomes less about fixing the past and more about expanding our ability to stay present with what is now, the discomfort as well as the lighter moments, and inevitably back again.

CHAPTER 15
The Four Colors of a Family System

In our journey to heal from sexual harm as a family or as a chosen family, it has been helpful to assign new words to refer to the roles each loved one plays within the social system. It is a rubric meant to bring us beyond the labels of victim, offender, and bystander, that only describe someone's relationship to the harm event in a limited way.

Rather than relying on terms that can feel inherently confrontational or passive, and dividing the system into victims and allies against perpetrators and their enablers, we can address all "loved ones" who are willing to commit to the work of healing, regardless of their relationship to the harm events.

Our language is a key part of how we undertake to rebalance the family system after sexual harm has occurred and ended. Within this framework, a person earns the honor of identifying with one of the four colors by committing to being a force for healing, both in their own life and in the lives of their loved ones.

Embracing a color signifies a lifelong commitment to the work associated with that role. This commitment extends beyond the point where harm reactions may fade from the family's daily life. It is an ongoing dedication to provide insight, accountability, and support wherever needed. Not just within our families, but in any context where our experiences can contribute to healing and safety within our spheres of influence.

From this point on, we will use these colors to describe anyone with a particular relationship to the harm who is actively engaged in the healing path. The colors honor both the individual's experience and their commitment to taking responsibility for their role in supporting a system impacted by child sexual abuse.

This color framework has proven to be a helpful shorthand to understand how we all fit into the healing process. Its neutral language allows us to see that our positions are not fixed.

Green

The Mighty Warriors: Those who were sexually harmed as children or young people who embody immense courage by standing up, refusing to let the harm remain in the shadows. The bravery of GREEN often ignites the conversations and provides the spark for the actions that set the family on a path toward healing. By facing the harm head-on, they encourage others to step forward and help build a safer, more supportive environment.

Blue

The Leading Upstanders: These are the loved ones who were also harmed by the events. Once they understand their own healing, they lend their strength and perspective to the healing path for others, and the system as a whole. Often siblings, partners, or adult children, Blues play a pivotal role in challenging harmful dynamics and fostering a clearer understanding of boundaries. Whether through speaking up for change, encouraging accountability, or helping to rebuild trust, BLUEs' efforts are instrumental in shifting the family system toward greater stability.

Orange

The Powerful Engines: Non-offending parents and caregivers who choose to engage with the impact of past harm can shift the foundation of the entire family. When the ORANGES confront how the harm affected their own lives and allow space for the emotions that come with it, they model a different way forward. Their ability to reset the tone and culture of the family matters. Through clear boundaries, seeking support, or encouraging honest conversation, their efforts can reshape the system and lay the groundwork for prevention. By acknowledging the harm and refusing to look away, they bring their influence to bear on creating more fertile ground for change.

Purple

The Humble Stewards: Those who have caused sexual harm to a young person and are no longer at risk of repeating that behavior hold a vital and often unseen role in the work of healing. By holding space for the impact of their actions, the PURPLES help restore integrity to fractured relationships and environments. Their presence, grounded in responsibility rather than avoidance, can shift the atmosphere of a family or community. They offer stewardship for healing, safety, truth, and prevention. When embraced with care, their role becomes a source of healing for others—not despite the harm caused, but through their commitment to face it fully.

The Four Colors

These four colors represent the active roles we take within a family system or community in response to significant harm events. These roles are not passive; they require strength, intentionality, and an ongoing commitment. Simply having this as a personal experience does not grant someone the right to identify with a particular color. Instead, it is the commitment to actively engage in the healing process and in preventing future harm that defines the identity with a particular color.

In this framework, there is an equal seat at the table for all who step onto the path of healing. Each color brings a unique perspective, its own set of struggles, and specific strengths to the process. Together, they form the foundation for meaningful repair. By understanding and honoring these roles as parts of a greater whole, we cultivate a fuller and more integrated picture of what restoration might be.

CHAPTER 16

The Green Experience

> **Green:** Adults who have experienced sexual abuse under the age of 25 who are actively working to overcome the lasting impacts of that trauma on their lives and relationships.

The path to healing from the GREEN experience demands immense courage. Few realities are as difficult to face—within ourselves or in the people we love—as the impact of child sexual abuse. Like other forms of trauma, it defies easy explanation. Words often fail to capture its depth, its reach, or its aftermath. And yet, those who identify as GREEN are asked to do what feels impossible: to confront what was done to them, name it for themselves, and find a way forward in a world that often looks the other way.

This chapter is not an attempt to define the experience of every person who identifies as GREEN. Each GREEN carries a story shaped by their own relationships, circumstances, and survival instincts. Their path is deeply personal and must remain self-defined. Instead, this chapter is written as a guide for those who love someone who has been sexually harmed in their youth. Through what I've learned, both from my own personal experiences of sexual harm and from walking alongside hundreds of GREENS, I hope to offer insight that builds understanding, strengthens support, and deepens empathy.

This chapter may also resonate with GREENS seeking language for what has felt inexpressible, or affirmation that they are not alone. The goal is not to explain their experience to them but to offer a framework that honors the depth of their reality while helping others see more clearly what they cannot fully know.

Sexual harm before the age of twenty-five reaches into every corner of a person's being. It strikes during the most formative years when identity is still forming, and a sense of self-in-the-world is still taking shape. Unlike harm experienced in adulthood, childhood and adolescent sexual abuse disrupts development from the inside out. The impact is not just emotional or physical. It is developmental, relational, and often invisible to those who don't have this as a personal experience, and often for those that do.

Too often, we make the mistake of projecting adult thinking onto a child's mind, assuming they understood what was happening, or how it would impact them, in the same way we would now, as adults. To truly grasp the impact of sexual harm, we must consider who the child was at the time, their cognitive, emotional, and spiritual capacities, and how those were altered in the aftermath. That's the only way we begin to see the full picture of what it means to live the GREEN experience.

Family members and friends might find themselves thinking or saying things like:

> *"Why didn't they tell anyone, if it was so horrible?"*
> *"At 15 years old, he was big enough to fight back."*
> *" It happened so long ago. Enough already."*
> *"Children sometimes play that way."*
> *"At least it wasn't rape!"*
> *"How many times do I have to say I am sorry?"*

"If they could only forgive, then everything would be ok."
"Are we never allowed to be happy as a family again?"
"I can't be blamed for what I didn't know."
"Don't they see how good their life is now?"
"What about how the rest of us are suffering?"
"You must have misunderstood their intentions."

While these comments often stem from confusion or good intentions, they can deepen the pain and disconnection for the GREEN. Hearing remarks like these can reinforce just how alone they feel, highlighting the distance between their lived experience and the incomplete, often misguided narrative of those around them.

It is understandable we want to see our loved one in a better place. It's human to want resolution, to hope that saying the right thing might somehow lift the weight for everyone. Unfortunately, healing doesn't come from being reasoned with, given a different way of seeing it or persuaded to forgive. And for the GREEN, these efforts often land as pressure, not support.

These common responses from our loved ones are usually born from frustration, a longing for relief, and uncertainty about how to find it. Family members want change but often don't know how to create it. And so the same conversations repeat, the same questions linger, and the same disconnection grows. For the GREEN, this dynamic is exhausting and pushes them deeper into despair.

Over time, this sense of limbo can wear down even the most well-meaning family members. Hope gives way to resignation. Relationships that once felt close begin to drift, until silence replaces connection. All the while, the GREEN is left holding the burden of both the original harm and the system's inability to understand it.

From the outside, it may look like the GREEN is stuck sabotaging relationships, avoiding progress, or clinging to the past. At times, they may appear to be doing well, only to abruptly leave a marriage, lose a job, or fall into a deep depression. Others may seem like superstars, high-functioning and successful, but when their inner world is revealed, the suffering is raw and unrelenting. These moments can confuse and overwhelm the family members, intensifying the feelings of helplessness.

Until family members better understand the nature and impact of sexual harm, their attempts to help will often miss the mark. What the GREEN needs is not advice, logic, or encouragement to "see the good in their life," but the steady presence of people willing to learn, listen, and stay through the discomfort.

Understanding Soul Loss

To understand why the effects of sexual harm are so difficult to overcome, we need to understand what I will call *soul loss*. This concept helps explain the deep, often invisible wounds left by the shame event. It can help us understand why its impact extends far beyond the initial trauma and continues to shape every aspect of a person's life.

When a child experiences a betrayal such as sexual harm, whether by a trusted adult or another minor, their sense of innocence and openness can be profoundly disrupted. Safety, once taken for granted, becomes something they must monitor and manage for themselves. Being used for someone else's sexual gratification doesn't just damage trust in the person who caused harm. It fractures trust in all the adults who were supposed to protect them.

When that faith is broken early, the inner dialogue shifts: *Am I really alone? Am I unworthy of protection? Is it up to me to stay safe*? I've heard countless survivors say, "I raised myself." Not because no one fed them or enforced a bedtime, but because, deep down, they felt solely responsible for their own safety—even if they couldn't have named it at the time.

When innocence and self-worth are replaced by adaptations like hyper-vigilance, emotional withdrawal, manipulation, or carefully managed personas, that is *soul loss*. The part of the self that once trusted in care goes into hiding. What remains is a version of the self built to endure.

These adaptations are not weaknesses. They are protective strategies shaped by survival. They can show up in countless ways: as the straight-A student striving for control or validation, or the teen skipping school to smoke pot in the parking lot. Some regress into dependency, while others become fiercely independent, refusing to rely on anyone. They might take extreme risks or stay rigidly inside their comfort zones. One person might push others away with anger, while another becomes the life of the party—charming, agreeable, and impossible to truly know.

Over time, these strategies can harden into fixed personality traits. What once served to keep the child safe becomes how the adult is seen and sometimes how they see themselves. Vulnerability, openness, and trust are often sacrificed to maintain the protective identity and continue to show up as others expect. As the GREEN grows older, this can compromise their ability to form authentic relationships. They become harder to reach.

Beneath it all, *soul loss* leaves behind a deep and often wordless shame. Even if the GREEN can't name it, or they believe in the worth they earn through their accomplishments, it lingers, reshaping how they move through the world and what they believe they deserve.

It quietly limits how much of themselves they share, and with whom. Resentment builds as they struggle to maintain the person they think they need to be, for their own safety or to maintain their relationships. And yet, many reach a moment, a breaking point or a slow awakening, when they realize: *"I don't want to live like this anymore."* That recognition, however it comes, marks the beginning of reclaiming what was lost.

Soul loss is not self-correcting; the parts of the self set aside in moments of danger don't automatically return when safety does. Reclaiming them requires effort, awareness, and a willingness to confront long-standing patterns. While *soul loss* is not unique to sexual abuse, it can occur in any unsafe environment that overwhelms a child's natural coping mechanisms. It is a defining feature of childhood sexual harm.

For family members and loved ones, understanding the impact of sexual harm allows us to see these patterns not as flaws, but as evidence of survival. When we recognize that *soul loss* was an incredible adaptation to an unjust experience, we can meet it with more patience, empathy, and clarity.

***A Green Story**: Love of Soccer*

Scotty's world was a blur of letters and numbers that danced mockingly across the page, his dyslexia turning each school day into a grueling battle. But on the soccer field, everything changed. There, he was grace in motion, his feet moving with a surety his mind could never match in the classroom. Recess and after-school clubs became his sanctuary, the place where he could shine.

In fourth grade, Scotty's talent caught the eye of his coach, a man who saw beyond the struggling student to the gifted athlete within. "This boy has raw talent," he told Scotty's parents, his eyes alight with possibility. "With the right coaching, he could go far." The coach spoke of a prestigious training camp, a golden opportunity that Scotty's parents couldn't ignore, despite the financial strain it would place on their modest income.

At the camp, Scotty felt like he'd found his true home. The thud of the ball against his foot, the rush of wind as he sprinted across the field, it all felt right in a way nothing else ever had. He forged close bonds with his coaches and teammates, feeling more open from belonging to this special group. For the first time in his young life, Scotty felt truly proud of himself.

One night, as laughter echoed through the bunks

and Scotty basked in the camaraderie of his friends, one of the younger coaches appeared in the doorway. "Scotty," he called casually, "come with me. I want to show you something." Trusting without hesitation, Scotty jumped up and followed his coach out into the evening air.

He could not have comprehended the sexual harm this coach inflicted on him. Nothing prepared him for anything like this, and when he was feeling so open and free, it hurt him even more. The coach told him if he tried to tell someone, they wouldn't believe him, and he would ensure that Scotty never played soccer again.

Scotty was never going to tell anyone anyway. He had lost soul parts that lived in him, the parts that felt proud of himself, close to his friends, open to the adults around him, and safe. He used to think he was special, and now what was left in him was suspicion that "special" actually meant vulnerable to getting taken advantage of. What was left after that rape, was self blame, anger and a decidedly strong unwillingness to ever trust anyone again.

The next morning, Scotty woke to a world that had shifted dramatically. The look on his face spoke volumes. His coaches kept asking him if he was OK. He would grunt something and then run off to chase down the ball even harder. His friends tried to get him to laugh, and join in but he started to remove himself from group activities. He became watchful, avoiding the coach who had harmed him, losing sleep at night, and skipping meals.

In the weeks that followed, the memory of that night slipped deeper into the recesses of Scotty's mind, burrowing into the cracks of his consciousness. But while the details faded, they left behind a pervasive sense of brokenness, a feeling that something fundamental within him had been irreparably damaged.

Back home, Scotty threw himself into soccer with a newfound intensity. The field became both his refuge and his battleground, a place where he could channel the anger and self-loathing that now simmered constantly beneath the surface. His plays became more aggressive, fueled by a desperate need to prove his worth, to be "enough."

Scotty's transformation didn't go unnoticed. His parents watched with a mixture of pride and concern as their once-carefree son became a driven, often sullen young man. The sweet boy who had once been surrounded by friends now kept to himself, his former companions left bewildered by his sudden withdrawal.

As Scotty ascended through the ranks of competitive soccer, eventually securing a coveted spot on a top Division One college team, his parents beamed with pride. But beneath their smiles lay a current of worry, a nagging sense that something had been lost along the way. They celebrated their son's achievements, unaware of the heavy price he was paying with silence, the invisible scars he had been carrying that altered his personality.

In the roar of the crowd and the glory of his athletic accomplishments, Scotty found a temporary respite from the darkness within. In the quiet moments, he hated to be with his thoughts, though not fully understanding why. The loss of innocence, openness and trust transformed him into a closed, vigilant, more angry person who became a driven accomplished athlete, and someone who was never harmed by that coach or anyone else ever again, but at great cost to the other aspects of who he might have been.

Scotty's transformation didn't go unnoticed. His parents watched with a mixture of pride and concern as their once-carefree son became a driven, often sullen young man. The sweet boy who had once been surrounded by friends now kept to himself, his former companions left bewildered by his sudden withdrawal.

As Scotty ascended through the ranks of competitive soccer, eventually securing a coveted spot on a top Division One college team, his parents beamed with pride. But beneath their smiles lay a current of worry, a nagging sense that something had been lost along the way. They celebrated their son's achievements, unaware of the heavy price he was paying with silence, the invisible scars he had been carrying that altered his personality.

In the roar of the crowd and the glory of his athletic accomplishments, Scotty found a temporary respite from the darkness within. In the quiet moments, he hated to be with his thoughts, though not fully understanding why. The loss of innocence, openness and trust transformed him into a closed, vigilant, more angry person who became a driven accomplished athlete, and someone who was never harmed by that coach or anyone else ever again, but at great cost to the other aspects of who he might have been.

The Role of Cognitive Development

To fully process and integrate traumatic experiences, we need a framework for understanding them. Normally young people do not have this understanding. In response, they develop strategies and skills to manage overwhelming emotions. These coping mechanisms can take many common forms. Some may appear positive on the surface, like Scotty's athletic achievements, while others may be more subtly or visibly destructive.

Regardless of their outward appearance, these strategies serve as lifelines, enabling young people to navigate their pain and reach adulthood intact. Until GREENS achieve some level of adult cognitive development, they may struggle to articulate or fully comprehend the shame event and resulting harm that has shaped their experiences. Even well into adulthood, many continue to struggle with understanding and accepting the impact of the abuse they endured.

This struggle is neither a personal failing nor a sign of dishonesty; it is a natural consequence of trauma intersecting with a still-developing mind. The ability to speak about the abuse often emerges later, as cognitive maturity allows for a more nuanced and comprehensive understanding of what occurred. When someone reaches the point where they are ready to talk about their experiences, it marks a decisive moment in their healing journey. Until that moment, survival takes precedence.

Why Memories Come Later

Secrecy around sexual abuse is deeply corrosive. Even when the victim doesn't consciously remember the events, their body and mind may respond to unconscious triggers in the present. When the harm remains unspoken or unacknowledged, it often feeds a persistent and false belief: *There is something wrong with me.* Keeping the abuse hidden, consciously or not, drains emotional energy and reinforces internalized shame. Until the memories are brought into the light and given voice, they will continue to cause harm.

One of the most bewildering aspects of sexual harm for family members can be that the memories often don't surface until years, even decades, later. This delay is not uncommon. In fact, research shows that, on average, it takes between 17 and 24 years for a survivor to disclose childhood sexual abuse. These delays are influenced by many factors, including the survivor's age at the time of the abuse, their relationship to the offender, and whether they had safe and supportive people to turn to.

The reasons for delayed disclosure are complex and rarely rooted in deception. Often, young people lack the vocabulary to describe what's happening to them. Without language to describe in a way an adult would understand what is happening, they struggle to get the support they need. Many survivors recall trying to tell a parent or caregiver what was happening. Considering how upsetting sexual harm to a child is, many adults dismiss what is being said or avoid it entirely.

A child might say someone gives them a stomachache, describe an adult as "weird" or "creepy," or ask for a lock on their bedroom door. They may become extremely upset when they are going to be left with the offender. These may seem like small things, but they can be early warning signs.

Unfortunately, adults don't always get curious enough to dig deeper and ask more direct questions. Sometimes this is due to a lack of awareness about the prevalence and nature of child sexual abuse. Other times, the adult's own unresolved trauma prevents them from seeing the warning signs.

In some cases, the adult recognizes that something inappropriate has occurred and takes steps to address it. They may confront the offender, ensure the child's immediate safety, or put protections in place for other children. But they may never return to the child to help them process what happened, believing that not talking about it is somehow better. This silence can be deeply confusing for the child, who is left alone to make sense of the experience and what it means about them.

There are also parents or caregivers who, because of their own histories of sexual harm or deep feelings of guilt for placing the child in harm's way, unconsciously distance themselves from the truth. They may minimize, deny, or even blame the child as a way of managing their own shame and fear. This deepens the rupture.

Later, when the GREEN begins to piece together what happened in adulthood, this second layer of betrayal of realizing no one helped them name or hold the truth, can be another aspect of the overall harm.

When direct or indirect signs of harm go unnoticed, the mind often suppresses or disconnects from the memory entirely. However, the effects of the trauma continue to play out in behaviors, relationships, and mental health, even when the original events remain inaccessible to the consciousness.

Understanding this helps explain why disclosure often comes late and why the pain may seem to surface suddenly and then shift quickly. For family members, it's important to know that this is not unusual. Moving in and out of memories, cycling through levels of pain, or having wide variations in how the harm is remembered or understood are all common experiences for GREENS.

This is not a way to determine how serious the harm was. It's a reflection of how deeply the mind worked to protect the child, even from their own awareness. When those memories begin to be spoken out loud, it means safety has finally reached a level where knowing becomes possible. And that, too, is part of the healing.

Reclaiming Our Agency

As GREENS reach a stage where self-determination feels more secure, they may begin to confront the harm they endured. This decision often arises alongside a growing sense of safety in their current life. The first step is often disclosure which is a courageous act signalling a readiness to engage with the truth and allow relationships to evolve.

Sometimes, it's a step toward closeness. Other times, it marks the beginning of separation. Either way, disclosure is rarely a single event. It's a layered, vulnerable process; one in which long-buried experiences begin to surface, and the individual begins to externalize their pain.

For family members and loved ones, the most supportive response is one of care, compassion, and respect for the GREEN's lived experience as they currently understand it. This can be difficult, especially when emotions run high or the details feel confusing. If we focus on the impact and emotional truth of what's being shared rather than trying to dissect or verify the facts, we're far more likely to be helpful. We can't undo what happened, but we can create an environment that supports the GREEN as they move forward at their own pace.

This process is about reclaiming agency, processing trauma, and weaving these experiences into a fuller understanding of the self. It is deeply personal work only the individual can do. A supportive environment can make all the difference. It allows the GREEN to explore their memories and their meaning on their own terms.

At this stage, the goal is not to establish certainty about every detail. Trauma memories, especially those formed in early childhood, often return in fragments, and may shift over time. What matters is acknowledging the pain being shared and recognizing the weight of carrying it alone.

When a non-offending parent hears their child's disclosure and responds with, "That couldn't have happened," they miss a powerful opportunity to offer support. Their inability to take in the information in that moment is understandable but extremely hurtful and most likely a set back. Even if the details are hard to process, being present for the emotional truth is what matters most. That said, we can usually go back and repair.

It is worth noting that while false reports do occur, they are estimated at around 2% of cases reported to authorities. Only 12% of cases are reported to the authorities, so you can imagine what a small fraction that is.

If the overwhelming majority of disclosures are genuine, insisting on proof distracts from the real work of healing and undermines trust in the relationship. As the GREEN continues to recall and integrate their memories, their story may change. That is common. What they need from loved ones is not certainty, but steadiness.

Someone who will stay with them through the emotional discomfort of healing from harm, when they remember perfectly and when the fog sets in. A support person who knows that the memories will come together as they do, when they do, if they ever do but the body knows what it has been through.

Healing is never linear. GREENS may move between empowerment and struggle. They may pause, pull back, or seem to disengage entirely. These shifts are not signs of failure or disinterest in getting better. They are part of the natural rhythm of recovery.

Resist the temptation to reference moments when they "seemed better" or appeared close to the person who caused harm. Progress often happens in quiet moments when something internal shifts, when insight settles, when rest gives space for growth. And then, back again, another dip in the ground. All of this is part of the process.

Many GREENS find as they move forward, they rediscover parts of themselves they thought were lost. The ultimate goal is to reach a place where the harm no longer defines one's life. Where joy and ease return to the one who was harmed. It isn't about reconciliation with any particular person, just a sense that they are back on their feet, living the life they want.

To the family members reading this: thank you for your willingness to learn and care. You may not hear gratitude from your GREEN right away, but your effort to understand the lifelong impact of sexual harm to a young person matters. It sets change in motion, often in ways you cannot yet see.

CHAPTER 17

The Blue Experience

Blue: The loved ones - typically siblings, intimate partners, and adult children - who have been impacted by the sexual abuse that occurred within their family system and wants to participate in the healing.

Blues are the overlooked victims in the aftermath of sexual abuse. They stand in the blast radius of the harm, absorbing shockwaves that alter their lives in ways both subtly masked and routinely unacknowledged. As collateral damage, these family members are often left to pick up the pieces, navigate tangled family dynamics, or suppress their own needs in the shadow of others' more visible pain.

This represents a missed opportunity for family healing. By virtue of their position, BLUES often hold a rare combination of emotional connection and relative stability. They are close enough to feel the family's pain in a visceral way, yet distant enough to offer a more grounded perspective. This dual awareness can serve as a powerful catalyst for change within the family system. When supported and empowered, BLUES frequently become key players in reshaping family dynamics and advancing collective healing.

In this chapter, we'll explore four distinct BLUE experiences: a sibling to a GREEN, an intimate partner to a GREEN, an adult child to a GREEN, and an intimate partner to a PURPLE. Each story reveals a unique dimension of the BLUE role, shedding light on the challenges, responsibilities, and opportunities for growth that come with their place in the family constellation.

A Blue Story: *The Super-Sister*

Astrid's path to becoming a social worker was shaped by her childhood experiences. Her mother's cousin, who often babysat, began sexually abusing her younger brother, Jonah, when he was about 5 years old. The abuse occurred at night, unbeknownst to Astrid or her parents at the time.

As her brother withdrew emotionally Astrid, who was five years older, found herself increasingly taking responsibility for his well-being. His anxiety became severe, impacting his ability to attend school or socialize. Astrid was frequently called upon to manage his panic attacks at school and at home, often at the expense of her own education and social life. Jonah would only be soothed by his sister.

By middle school, there was a daily fight between Jonah and their parents as he refused to go to school. The parents, overwhelmed and frustrated, delegated his morning routine to Astrid, as she was the only one who could get him out the door to school. She managed his schoolwork and made excuses for his absences, facing pressure from school administrators.

The situation escalated when Jonah began using marijuana in high school, ostensibly to manage his anxiety. Astrid, who was attending the local college, was trying to get her own life underway but her parents really needed her living at home to manage her brother. Jonah was beginning to spiral out of control. He went from pestering his parents for money, to threatening them.

The family was fracturing despite her best efforts to mediate a solution. The crisis peaked when his mother said she would not give him any more money. She said "get a job if you need drug money". This escalated the conflict, and Jonah pulled a knife from the kitchen drawer. His mother handed him her purse and when he left, she called the police.

Jonah was placed in psychiatric in-patient care. After many months, the parents and Astrid were called in for a family session. During the session, Jonah, without looking up, described how their mother's cousin would come into his room at night and force him to perform sexual acts.

When he finished and glanced up at his mother's face, she looked incredulous, then stood up, visibly shaking and said, "I am so sick of your excuses and lies." She stormed out, their father following behind.

They never spoke of what Jonah had said again, not when he came home, and not when he eventually moved out. Astrid didn't bring it up either; she didn't know how. Their parents carried a deep resentment toward Jonah and seemed relieved when he was finally on his own.

Astrid stayed by his side.

Jonah had no idea how to take care of himself.

He didn't have a high school diploma and had never held a job. Though the medication helped and he'd stopped smoking pot, he continued to struggle. Astrid took many late-night calls, driving to pick him up or helping him navigate conflict with a landlord, neighbor, or coworker.

By the time Jonah reached adulthood, he was barely managing. He worked a low-wage job and lived alone in a small apartment. Astrid was his lifeline. Their parents rarely spoke to him and only included him in family gatherings when Astrid insisted.

Tragically, her brother died in his late twenties of an overdose.

The Blue Sibling:

BLUES often take on responsibilities far beyond their years or position within the family system. Astrid's story exemplifies this premature assumption of adult duties. From a young age, she became her brother's primary caregiver and the reliable stabilizer for her parents. Her sacrifice to her own childhood seemed to go largely unnoticed.

The emotional labor BLUES perform is intense and multifaceted. They often become the steady presence in a household rocked by trauma, expected to keep moving forward without much support. Whether it's the sexual harm itself, the acting out or acting in of the GREEN or the family's fractured response to it (or all of the above) BLUES are affected in ways that often go unseen.

BLUE siblings are often young themselves. They can become parentified at a young age. By understanding they need to both stay out of the way and help, many learn to meet their own needs quietly, careful not to add to the chaos. Parents, desperate for something to feel okay, often look at the BLUE and think, *Thank God at least one of them is doing well.* As a result, they are reinforced for this behavior.

To see them as either unharmed or unaffected by years of family struggle is a mistake. BLUES carry a different kind of weight. They are secondary victims of the sexual harm event. They are often shaped by the ongoing pressure to hold things together, the guilt and anger that feels unacceptable to express, and the helplessness of not knowing what to do.

Over time, the caretaking tendencies that helped them manage their family life can become core to their identity. Always scanning for what others need. Always the helper, the fixer, the one who doesn't burden others. This can be exhausting and compromise their own relationships. Many BLUES learn to rely mostly on themselves.

That's why it matters when family members, including the GREEN, make the effort to ask: *How did the sexual harm impact you? How are you doing now?* Keep asking. It might take time for a BLUE to believe it's safe to speak honestly.

A Blue Story: *The Struggling Spouse*

John and Maria's relationship began in college on the East Coast, far from Maria's small town roots in Western Canada. After graduation, they settled on the East Coast, with Maria seemingly content to distance herself from her hometown.

Their infrequent visits back were marked by an undercurrent of tension that John couldn't quite place. Her family never seemed interested in visiting them. Despite his efforts to connect with his in-laws, he always sensed unspoken issues lingering beneath the surface.

Maria's pregnancy triggered a severe depression, forcing her to take leave from work. She would lay on the couch, while the baby cried in the other room. John was concerned about her ability to cope with parenthood. He sought professional help, arranging therapy and consulting doctors about medication options. John felt overwhelmed and confused by the escalating situation.

One night, it took a long time to get the baby to sleep. When he came out of the room, he found his wife curled up on the floor sobbing. "I don't think I can do this." He sat down next to her and waited for the crying to subside. He then said, "What happened? You were the one who pushed us to have a baby. I just can not understand what is happening."

After a long pause, she revealed that she had been sexually abused by her father and brother for many years. Now, she feels terrified that she will not be able to keep the baby safe. This disclosure shocked John. While he knew something was up with that family, he never would have guessed that.

He didn't know what to say, and while he ran over this information in his mind, she fell asleep. It was the first good night's sleep she had had in weeks. He, on the other hand, tossed and turned. He was awake all night flooded with different thoughts and emotions. The next morning when she woke up, he told her he was going to call her parents and brother.

This intention was met with Maria's vehement refusal. She started yelling that she should have never told him. Maria had never even considered talking to her family about the harm. She wanted to take it to her grave. She insisted this was her decision and hers alone, and she wanted to leave it in the past.

John felt emasculated, helpless and extremely confused by her desire to leave this unaddressed. He felt like he didn't have a voice because her emotions were running so high, and it was her family after all.

She made him promise to never talk about it to anyone, which he honored to his own detriment. Years passed, and this unspoken harm sat heavily between them. When they did visit her family, it left him feeling sick as he watched everyone bend over backward to be polite to one another. Upon returning home from a visit, his wife would crawl into bed and not come out for a week.

The Blue Partner to Green:

Unlike BLUES who grew up within the family system where the abuse occurred, John enters as an adult outsider, initially unaware of the trauma shaping his wife's life. The disclosure of Maria's abuse is a turning point. It not only marks a step in her healing but also pulls John into the family's hidden history, transforming him from bystander to potential ally.

Supporting Maria through her recovery means John must hold a complex balance between respecting her boundaries, shielding their children from potential harm, and managing his own emotional response to the abuse. The expectation that he remain steady, composed, and deferential to her lead can feel impossible. He too is impacted. For John, the negative consequences on his life come not from the harm event but the aftermath it leaves in its wake.

Before John can fully step into the role of ally, Maria must allow space for his secondary harm typical of the BLUE partner. Asking him to suppress his reactions in order to protect hers misses an opportunity for them to face the impact together.

When BLUE partners like John are given room to feel, speak, and act from their own truth, the burden of healing begins to shift from resting solely on the survivor to being shared in relationship. Together, Maria and John can set boundaries, protect their children, and foster healthier interactions within the family system—all while avoiding unnecessary and potentially harmful confrontations with others.

Ultimately, empowering BLUES to fully embrace their own experiences and feelings redistributes the burden of healing, lifting it from the Green alone. When the Blue partners are given a full seat at the table, acknowledged as individuals who are also deeply affected by the harm, they become active participants in the healing process rather than passive sideline supporters.

This shift introduces a valuable ally into the effort. By embracing their unique role and acknowledging their impact, Blue partners move from bystanders to participants who help drive progress, fostering a more resilient and balanced family dynamic for future generations.

A Blue Story*: Uncle with Answers*

Joseph's childhood was marked by instability and fear. His parents' relationship was volatile, with frequent arguments escalating to physical violence. Both parents drank excessively, their mood swings were unpredictable. Joseph often witnessed one parent storming out after a fight, threatening never to return. Days would pass before they came home, leaving Joseph in a constant state of uncertainty.

As he grew older, Joseph found himself stepping into a parental role. He'd intervene in their fights, confiscating bottles and sending his parents to bed as if he were the adult. This role reversal bred resentment in Joseph, as he struggled with his parents' dysfunctional relationship.

During Joseph's high school years, his father's younger brother came to visit. His affable Uncle Steve sat back observing as the night went on, and the drinking increased. He saw Joseph's efforts to maintain peace in the household, and his embarrassment and shame that his parents acted like this in front of his uncle.

One evening, after Joseph's parents had gone to bed, Steve joined Joseph out on the porch. He was obviously annoyed and ashamed of his parents' behavior. Steve sat for a while just looking out into the backyard with Joseph, patting him knowingly on the back.

After a while he offered, "I see what you're going through with your parents. Your dad didn't have it easy growing up after our father died." He sat for a minute contemplating whether to go on, and tell his teenage nephew the whole story.

Joseph listened intently as his uncle explained how their mother made Joseph's father sleep in her bed, treating him as a spouse rather than a son. Steve said, "He was the oldest, and she relied on him for everything. It was unfair to do this to a boy still only 13 years old."

A strained silence fell between them. Joseph's uncle, noting his nephew's confusion, continued carefully, "Our mother sexually abused your father for years. It's why he drinks so much, why he sometimes explodes with anger at you and your mother. It's why he feels this overwhelming need to protect everyone, even when he can barely protect himself."

Joseph froze as this revelation settled over him. He felt a complex mix of emotions. There was comfort in understanding the reason his family felt so dysfunctional and also in having an adult acknowledge the burden he had been carrying. Yet, alongside that relief was a deep sadness and a new awareness of anger, though he wasn't quite sure what to do with it yet.

Sitting there with his uncle he felt so grateful to have this information, and a way to comprehend his family through new eyes. He teared up with compassion.

The Blue Child:

The next generation inherits not the direct harm but the aftermath, filtered through their grandparents, parents, and aunts/uncles' struggles. Children often internalize the dysfunction they do not understand. Developmentally they can only imagine they are the cause of it. Joseph was fortunate to have his uncle see what he was going through, acknowledge it and explain with compassion the origins of his behavior.

When the truth of family trauma surfaces a generation or more later, it casts a stark light on a lifetime of experiences. A parent's inexplicable anger, the threats to leave followed by silent returns, unspoken family tensions, or the mysterious relative who is never present and infrequently mentioned. All these fragments of the way it has always been suddenly take on new meaning when the next generation starts to understand a past before they were born.

This delayed understanding can feel both liberating and overwhelming, providing clarity while challenging long-held perceptions of family narratives and relationships. It demands a reckoning with the past and a reframing of the present, as adult children work to piece together the impact of inherited trauma they may never fully understand.

Adult children often serve as an inter-generational bridge. They are uniquely positioned to facilitate healing conversations that reach back to the ancestors. Their dual perspective—intimate knowledge of family dynamics coupled with the emotional distance that comes from not being subjected to direct harm—allows them to approach entrenched issues with both empathy and objectivity.

Blues from younger generations have the potential to bring transformative change to their families as they grow older and into adulthood. As they gain their own agency, they are more able to unpack the impact that the aftermath has had on them personally. They must untangle the distortions in the family lore that have held the past in a way that does not support healing. Once they can, they start to speak out loud creating a new paradigm for understanding the past harm.

***A Blue Story**: Married to Purple*

Parker cradled her newborn son, marveling at his tiny fingers and toes. Her husband, Mike, stood nearby, beaming with pride. Their family felt complete, a picture of happiness and new beginnings. The family members were stopping by the hospital to congratulate them both.

A few weeks later, their world shattered when Parker opened an email from Mike's cousin, Olivia. A family member she knew and loved. The message detailed the abuse she had endured as a young kid, sexually taken advantage of by her older cousin Mike. The email ended with a sarcastic: "I think you should know that your husband is a pedophile. Oh, and congrats on your new baby. Best of luck with that."

Olivia's words unraveled a painful family history her husband and every one of her in-laws kept from her. When Mike was 12 and Olivia was 8, he had sexually abused her. The incidents, spanning several years, had left a lasting wound on Olivia's life. She spoke openly about her eating disorder throughout her teens and twenties, connecting her struggle directly to the abuse.

Parker's mind reeled. The man she loved, the father of her child, suddenly seemed like a stranger. In a whirlwind of anger and fear, she asked Mike to leave their home. He went, devastated and confused, his perfect life crumbling around him.

Mike had never told Parker about what happened with Olivia. In his mind, it was a terrible mistake from his childhood, completely disconnected from the man he had become. He wasn't attracted to children and had never considered harming anyone sexually apart from this time in his life with Olivia. In fact, those memories with Olivia had faded, filed away as a regrettable chapter of his immaturity and youth.

As days passed, Mike battled a storm of emotions. He felt misunderstood, angry at being labeled a pedophile when he knew that was not who he was. He also felt a crushing guilt. He realized that while he had moved on to a better, more stable life, Olivia had been silently carrying the weight of his actions for two decades. Every family gathering, every casual interaction - she had been there, hurting, while he remained oblivious.

Parker, too, was caught in an emotional whirlwind. She loved Mike, but how could she trust him now? She thought of their newborn son and felt a fierce need to protect him. Yet, she also remembered the kind, loving man she had married, who she dated for years before marrying. Could that man and the boy who had hurt Olivia truly be the same person?

After weeks of separation, Parker agreed to attend counseling with Mike. In their sessions, Mike struggled to articulate his feelings. "I know what I did was wrong," he said, his voice shaking. "But I was a kid too. I didn't understand the impact it would have. I'm not that person. I would never, ever harm someone sexually, nor have I since, especially not a child."

He paused, tears welling in his eyes. "I do see how my feelings don't erase what happened to Olivia. I thought it was behind us, but for her, it wasn't. I feel so horrible for not realizing, and putting her through all those times of family gatherings together. I've been so blind. I don't even know how to make things right for her."

As they worked through their feelings in therapy, Mike and Parker began to see a path forward. It wouldn't be easy. Trust had been broken, not just with the harm he caused in his youth, but with Mike's choice to keep this part of his past hidden from her. They knew they had a long road ahead rebuilding their relationship, finding a way to acknowledge and address Olivia's pain, and ensuring their own child grew up in a home filled with honesty, understanding, and respect for boundaries.

Mike's journey of accountability was just beginning. Parker had made a commitment to stand by him, as long as he put in the work to make things as right as he possibly could with his cousin. They were not sure how they would do that but they knew it was a path of humility, accountability and not minimizing what she has been going through ever since.

Not everyone in Parker's life supported her decision to stay in her marriage. She lost friends, and some family members decided Mike was no longer welcome in their homes. As a result, she saw them less often, feeling both excluded and understanding of their perspective. Attempts to explain why her husband's past harm did not reflect his present risk often fell on deaf ears.

She felt sad when they were asked to sit out some holidays from his family to give Olivia space to enjoy herself without feeling triggered by his presence. Through sensitive family members, Mike managed to get word to Olivia that if she ever wanted to talk to him, he would just listen without defending his actions. So far, she hasn't wanted to.

Parker doesn't regret her choice. She loves her husband and her family. They have found people in their lives that love and accept them. She sees the complexity of child sexual abuse in a new way, and sees the hard work Mike puts into being accountable. While she still remains vigilant for any denial or minimization of his behavior, she continues to observe him taking responsibility for his work and never pushing the family members to feel differently than they do.

The Blue Partner to Purple:

For individuals like Mike, who caused harm as a minor and have not engaged in abusive behavior since, the work ahead involves accountability, education, developing genuine remorse, and repairing relationships where possible. This is distinct from situations where someone remains at risk of causing harm or committed abuse as an adult and has done no work on themselves. In those cases, getting into recovery and ensuring the safety of others must come before any attempts at repair or reintegration into the family.

When a BLUE partner chooses to remain in relationship with a PURPLE, they take on a significant responsibility. This role demands more than quiet loyalty. It requires a refusal to defend harmful actions, push for forgiveness, or shift the focus to others as sources of pain. Whether through silence, deflection, or minimization, these responses only deepen the collective wound. They risk reinforcing the original harm rather than helping to repair it.

It's a challenging role, but one where the unique position of a BLUE can offer powerful leadership. Anyone who stands for truth, models compassion for the person who was harmed, and still supports the PURPLE in doing the hard work of repair becomes a vital force in the family's healing. When done well, their steady presence doesn't just help hold the PURPLE accountable, it creates space for everyone in the family to move forward.

This work takes time. In some cases, relationships may not fully recover. However, staying connected to someone who caused harm does not require hatred or harshness. What it *does* require is courage and a willingness to look directly at the truth and gently, consistently, call the PURPLE out of hiding.

With empathy and resolve, a BLUE can encourage them to face the impact of their choices, to take responsibility for their own healing, to make meaningful amends where possible, and to find ways to contribute to the safety and wellbeing of others..

BLUES—whether siblings, partners, adult children, extended family, or close friends—are not just bystanders in the aftermath of sexual harm. They hold a unique role as bridge-builders and truth-tellers, capable of shifting family dynamics toward healing.

There is no hierarchy of pain. Everyone affected carries part of the injury, and each person deserves the chance to heal. Healing also requires accountability for how we've responded to harm, and how our responses may have helped or hurt others.

BLUES often show up in unexpected places: neighbors, in-laws, best friends, even former partners. What unites them is their choice to engage, to stay present and resist the pull of silence, avoidance, and blame.

When we make space for BLUES to face their own pain and step into their role with honesty and care, we unlock a powerful force. Their clarity, empathy, and courage can begin to repair what harm has fractured, offering families the possibility of a different future.

CHAPTER 18

The Orange Experience

Orange: The non-offending parent (or other adult caregivers) of a young person who was harmed sexually, or who caused sexual harm to another young person or both, and wants to play a role in the healing process.

Learning that one's child has been involved in sexual harm is a metaphorical car crash for a parent. Everything we thought we knew is suddenly thrown into question. The aftermath of the disclosure shakes the foundation of family life, forcing us to reevaluate our history, reframe our memories, and doubt how we once understood ourselves and our relationships.

The pain that follows is raw and consuming. It can feel like an unbearable weight, pressing into every corner of our lives. In the face of such devastation, we each respond in different ways. Some of us turn to denial, unable to fully take in what has happened. Others leap into action, trying to restore a sense of control. Still others retreat inward, withdrawing from community and connection, unsure how to show up honestly with the people around us.

Beneath all these reactions often lies a profound sense of guilt. For non-offending parents, the perceived failure to protect our child from harm or to prevent them from causing it, leaves a wound that words cannot easily capture. Many of us identify strongly with our role as a parent. When confronted with the reality of child sexual abuse, this identity can feel threatened.

In response, we may instinctively try to protect ourselves from the full weight of the truth. It's tempting to explain away the harm, minimize it, or attempt to convince the victim to let it go. We may try to equate our pain or that of other people with the suffering of those directly involved in the shame event or to advocate for moving forward without looking back.

We may want to focus the conversation on ourselves, reminding others that we are not just someone who failed to prevent this but a good parent in many important ways. And while that is probably true, these protective instincts, if left unexamined, can prevent us from being what our family needs most; an engine to keep things heading toward honesty, accountability, and a willingness to face the discomfort head on.

Guilt, shame, grief, confusion, and heartbreak can overwhelm our emotional capacity. And when we don't tend to that pain—when we push it aside or let it shape our behavior without reflection—we risk becoming another source of harm. Not out of cruelty, but out of avoidance. Unprocessed pain can cause us to freeze, lash out, deflect, or prioritize our own need for comfort over the needs of the child who was harmed, or the one who caused the harm. These reactions are deeply human but when left unchecked, they can compound the trauma and make healing harder for everyone.

There is another way. When we choose to face the truth with courage. When we do the internal work, seek support, and take responsibility for how we show up, we become a powerful force for healing. Our steady presence becomes a signal to the rest of the family that transformation is possible. We model what it means to hold compassion and accountability side by side.

We don't have to be perfect. We just have to be willing. The commitment we make to our own healing is not separate from our family's recovery. It is the foundation of it.

The **Orange Healing Journey** asks us to walk a dual path: to recognize ourselves both as people harmed by the shame event (the GREEN PATH), and as family members who hold some accountability for them (the PURPLE PATH).

The Green Path on the Orange Journey involves confronting our own feelings of harm and betrayal. It offers an opportunity to work through pain, anger, and grief independently of other family members. We need time to examine our coping mechanisms and understand for ourselves both the impact of the harm and the path to healing. We, too, need validation for our internal experiences and, ultimately, the space to cultivate our own resilience.

The Purple Path on the Orange Journey calls us to face the impact we have had on our child, whether we failed to keep them safe, or failed to keep them from causing harm, or both. Even when prevention wasn't possible, the responsibility to protect still rested with us. This path asks us to take ownership for any harm caused, directly or indirectly, through our actions, inactions, or the reactions we regret.

Building Stability

Cultivating emotional stability as an ORANGE, particularly as a parent, is foundational to family healing. We must develop the internal resilience, clarity, and self-awareness needed to stay grounded. Our work is never about managing others' feelings or pushing for reconciliation. Instead, it's about becoming a steady presence as we hold space, remain hopeful, and help navigate the complexities of harm with integrity.

One of our primary responsibilities is to maintain strong, clear boundaries, especially when others attempt to blur or ignore them. Healing doesn't come from simply encouraging two family members to talk again or tolerate each other's presence at gatherings. Momentary positive interactions or appearances of peace are not necessarily indicators of repair. We can expect to see steps forward and back again. While these may be good signs, resist the temptation to imagine, "Finally, all is well." True healing takes time.

The GREEN is on their own path, and we must respect that journey fully. Our role is not to push them forward or urge reconciliation. ORANGES protect the GREEN by ensuring they are not pressured by others or placed in situations where their needs are competing with those of the family system. The GREEN's ability to participate in family life should never hinge on enduring the presence of the person who harmed them unless they choose it themselves. Nor should they have to tolerate conversations that feel invalidating to their lived experiences of harm. We must not ask them to trade the emotional stability they need to recover for family unity.

When we are the parent of a PURPLE, our job is not to respond with blame, isolation, or discipline in an effort to show we don't condone their actions. What the PURPLE needs most is love and support. They need to know their worth is not erased by what they've done. And, we encourage them to face the natural consequences of their behavior. This includes holding them back when they attempt to cross boundaries, shift blame, or downplay the harm they caused.

As ORANGE parents, we serve the family best when we understand the quiet power we hold: to lead by example, uphold boundaries, and insist on emotional honesty. Supporting both the GREEN and the PURPLE means honoring each of their paths without forcing alignment. This work requires patience, clarity, and the courage to sit with what remains unresolved.

Even if reconciliation never comes or certain relationships remain distant, our role is not to control outcomes or piece the family back together. It is to create the conditions for healing by doing our own, staying present and by trusting others to walk their path in their own time.

An Orange Story: The Dress Fitting

Maya had been working on it in therapy for years. Quietly. Carefully. Naming it. Untangling the memory from her body. She wasn't ready to tell her family yet. Maybe not ever. Then her brother, Noah, got engaged.

Lily was lovely. The kind of person who made everyone feel happy for him. They were a sweet couple, even Maya thought so. When Lily asked Maya to be a bridesmaid, Maya said yes without hesitation.

Something unsettling started to rise in her after that. Little things started getting under her skin: the texts about dresses, the group photos from the engagement party, the way Lily's mom would talk about what a catch Noah was. The past began to press in on her, and her sessions with her therapist became more about how to survive the wedding than whether she would ever tell.

Still, she had no plan to say anything until the day they went dress shopping and out to lunch. It was a sunny Saturday afternoon and everyone was exhausted from store and store trying on dresses. Lily, Maya, and their mothers were sitting at a café, discussing the dresses they had seen.

Everyone was so joyful, and somehow it just all felt wrong to Maya. Lily was laughing about how Noah wanted to wear blue sneakers, and her own mother looked proud. Maya felt her heart beating loudly.

She could hear them talking, but the words blurred. And then, all at once, she said it.

"Noah sexually abused me when I was little. I just

didn't want you to get married without knowing what he did."

The table went silent.

Her mother's hand stopped mid-scroll. Lily blinked. Maya stared at the salt shaker, trying to slow her breath.

"What are you talking about?" her mother asked, voice sharp, brittle. "That isn't true" she looked up at Lily and her mother to reassure them. Lily looked stunned, then cold. "You should've come to me privately," she said. "You didn't think your brother deserved to speak for himself?" She and her mother got up from the table and left.

Behind the scenes, they closed ranks. The story became that Maya had only been joking and that she had always been jealous of her brother. Lily asked her to step down as a bridesmaid, saying she wanted to enjoy her day without worrying about what Maya might say, or who she might say it to.

Maya became the girl who ruined lunch. The sister who made it about herself. The unstable one. Even though, privately, no one seemed surprised. There was a silence in her parents' reactions, a calm in Lily's approach, that told Maya she wasn't the only one who knew.

Navigating Green and Purple

When the GREEN and the PURPLE are siblings, and the harm occurred during childhood, the entire family system is deeply affected. Parents face the difficult task of staying connected to both children while honoring their distinct and often conflicting needs. This is not about mediating or "fixing" the sibling relationship, but about supporting each child to do their own work: healing, rebuilding trust, and when appropriate, taking responsibility for the harm. This delicate process requires ongoing reflection, patience, and care.

By prioritizing emotional safety, supporting individual healing, and acknowledging the impact of each person's actions, parents model how to navigate these complex dynamics with clarity and compassion. It is essential to distinguish between the unconditional love and worth we offer each child, and the challenging process of healing and accountability, which can bring discomfort and uncertainty. Making this distinction creates the conditions for meaningful progress.

If the PURPLE is unwilling to take responsibility or engage in the work of repair, these dynamics can grow more painful over time. The GREEN may feel unsafe, unheard, or even erased. When efforts at family healing stall, emotional divides deepen, and trust frays. Parents who focus solely on staying connected to the PURPLE without requiring accountability risk signaling that the status quo is more important than the well-being of the GREEN. While the impulse to care for all one's children is natural, doing so with clear expectations and boundaries is critical to any hope of healing.

This complexity often intensifies when the GREEN and PURPLE are cousins or close family friends. In these cases, other non-offending parents and significant adults bring their own reactions, and the broader web of relationships becomes even more intertwined. Misalignment, blame, or unresolved tension between the parents' generation can compound the harm and create instability for the young people involved.

The quality of the relationships between non-offending parents can either support or disrupt the healing process. It is possible for parents and caregivers to work together to resolve conflict among themselves and present a supportive team for the GREEN and PURPLE. To do so, they must respect the uniqueness of each child's internal world and avoid trying to collapse their experiences into a single narrative.

When adults tend to their own grief, guilt, or anger, ideally outside the children's view, and commit to doing their own healing work, they help create a more stable, trustworthy environment. Modeling healthy communication, boundaries, and repair reinforces the understanding that healing is possible, and that it is shared work.

Supporting the Green

For the GREEN, emotional safety must be the top priority, allowing them to engage with the family at a pace and level that feels manageable to them. They need to know that their parent or parents are unequivocally in their corner, advocating for their well-being without hesitation. This includes addressing difficult issues with the PURPLE and ensuring that family gatherings are structured with the GREEN's comfort and capacity in mind through every stage of healing.

Parents must avoid placing any pressure on the GREEN to reconcile with the person who harmed them. Reconciliation is a complex endeavor that takes time and is also a personal decision. It cannot be forced, nor does it need to be a part of the healing. If it is going to happen, it will only unfold on the GREEN's terms, in their own time.

The parent's role is not to push for the relationship to repair or lose sleep over connections that may never return. When we find ourselves thinking, *if only they could forgive, everything would be okay*, we must pause and remember: forgiveness is not the goal, healing is. Forgiveness is one of those false shortcuts that make the family feel better but are not necessarily an indicator of healing.

This viewpoint requires grieving the family dynamic that may never come back and learning to love each individual as best we can in a new way. Supporting the GREEN means honoring their boundaries, listening without defensiveness, and making it clear through actions, not just words—that their needs will not be compromised for the sake of family harmony.

Supporting the Purple

For the parent of PURPLE, the foundation of support lies in holding unwavering love and making it clear that we will not abandon them. At the same time, we firmly and with compassion, insist they face the natural consequences of their actions, which often include some form of exclusion, and take meaningful steps to understand how they came to cause sexual harm.

Shame is usually already present in abundance; it's not something we need to contribute to. When our PURPLE child retreats into Phase One coping strategies, such as denial, avoidance, or blaming others, we can recognize these as protective, though temporary, responses. And when they are ready, we encourage them to return to the work: facing the harm they caused, taking responsibility, and seeking the help they need to grow and, where possible, make amends.

Balancing love with clear boundaries shows the PURPLE that a path forward is possible. Healing from causing sexual harm is possible. Non-offending parents play a vital role in reminding the PURPLE that they, too, have a part to play for themselves, for their family, and sometimes even for the GREEN. In moments of hopelessness, we remind them that the work is lifelong, and the most important thing they can do is continue taking meaningful steps to counter their past behavior without losing sight of their own humanity.

The End of 'Business As Usual'

While specific responses will vary depending on the circumstances, one principle remains constant: once we know, we cannot go back to the way things were. As ORANGE parents, we recognize that everything shifted the moment we learned of the harm. Our role is now different, and it's our responsibility to reshape the family dynamic with clarity and compassion. This includes ensuring that no one is allowed to relate to the GREEN, the PURPLE, or the family as a whole as if nothing happened. Business as usual is over.

This shift often brings discomfort, especially when it comes to who knows and who does not. ORANGE parents regularly feel limited in what we can share because we do not feel it is our story to tell. It is not uncommon to feel caught between protecting our child's privacy and unsure how to relate to others, especially those who do not know. We may experience feelings of isolation because we can't freely share what we are going through even with those closest to us.

Both the GREEN and the PURPLE have a right to decide who hears their story and when, remembering that each narrative is individual. There is not one story of harm, but there is 'our story' of the harm. The ORANGE also has a story of their own. While we avoid sharing it with those who would impact the GREEN or the PURPLE in ways that will hurt them, we do need to speak about our grief, our confusion, our responsibility, the pain to someone safe. We are part of this story too, and voicing our truth in appropriate ways will eventually help us to show up for the family in supportive ways.

One of the most challenging times is when we carry the weight of what happened, but others in the family do not. When the PURPLE or GREEN are not ready to disclose to others, and actively ask us not to share, it can lead to a painful sense of inauthenticity. Birthdays, holidays, and phone calls with people who are unaware of the harm can be awkward. It is a powerful sign of healing when the GREEN or PURPLE choose to share their truth with others. Each time the story is disclosed, the shame gets lighter. With more people holding it, the weight lessens.

In some families, the GREEN and PURPLE may be part of the same family circle or there may be more than one GREEN. Often, one person is ready to speak openly about the harm before the others. These can be delicate times. Disclosure is an important part of healing, and we want to encourage it. When it is focused on personal healing, and not retaliation, we support it even when that causes us great discomfort. We do not stifle those who need to speak, but we do support them in doing so with sensitivity. As more people understand what happened, and as silence gives way to honest conversation, we can begin to expect more from the entire family system.

Reshaping the family after sexual harm is not about exposing secrets for shock value or picking sides. It is about refusing to participate in the illusion that nothing happened. The more honest we are, the more healing becomes possible. And while it may take time, ORANGE parents have the power to participate in this shift, not by force, but by modeling what it means to live in truth, hold boundaries, and remain connected.

***An Orange Story**: The Widow*

I sat across from Agnes, a woman in her early sixties, her hands twisting nervously in her lap. The weight of what we were about to discuss hung heavy in the air between us. Agnes had recently discovered that her late husband, Lars, had sexually abused their son, Jordan, for many years. The pain and disbelief in her eyes were palpable.

"I'm... I'm not sure if I believe him, Jordan that is," Agnes began hesitantly, her voice barely above a whisper. "It just doesn't seem possible." Shame was filling the room. She was glancing up at my face to see if I was judging her for saying that; I wasn't.

As I gently recounted some of the stories Jordan had shared with me, I watched Agnes's face contort. She winced, her eyes squeezing shut as if trying to physically block out the images my words conjured. My heart ached for her; the instinct to protect oneself from such painful truths is deeply human, and evident in her expression.

"Let's take a moment," I suggested softly. "Just breathe."

After a few deep breaths, Agnes began to speak again. She started to explain that Lars had a rough childhood, a landscape of insecurity. His father had been violent toward their mother and controlling of the children. As she told me stories of what he went through, I could see she was hoping I would embrace her late husband's humanity. Perhaps not see him as the kind of person who would harm a child sexually. Or at least let him off the hook for some of his shortcomings.

"He pulled himself out of that mess," she said, a note of pride creeping into her voice. "He became the CEO of a successful company. He provided for us, and paid for the kids' private school education. I was always so proud of who he had become considering what he had been through. Even after all of that, he always took care of his parents financially. They wanted for nothing, even though, in my mind, they deserved nothing."

I nodded, acknowledging her words. "Yes, I understand. No one can be summed up by their worst behavior alone. Lars sounds like he was a great man in many ways, and overcame a lot to become who he was." I was hoping to communicate in my tone 'yes, we can love someone and also confront the harm they have caused.'

A small smile flickered across Agnes's face. As she allowed herself to have this memory of her husband, a space opened up and what filled it was a more honest assessment of him. "How could he have done such a horrible thing? How could I have missed this? I must be such a horrible mother" Agnes's voice cracked, tears welling in her eyes.

I closed my eyes, feeling the weight of her pain. The devastation of discovering such a betrayal is immeasurable and overwhelming to the point that we just do not want that to be true. Trying to go back and reconstruct decades with this man, their marriage, their family, their intimate life. What does it all amount to through this new frame?

"What do I do?" Agnes's question seemed directed more at the universe than at me.

"I think you're doing it now," I replied gently. "You're beginning to let in the complexity of who he was. Facing this difficult truth happens in stages and overtime. In this moment, I see you slowly allowing yourself to feel the pain, the confusion, the anger. This is the first step towards healing, for you and for Jordan."

Adult Offenders We Love

Navigating sexual harm perpetrated by an adult loved one is among the most excruciating paths an Orange can walk, especially when the person who caused harm is still alive. The emotional landscape is thick with impossible choices. In some cases, there is financial dependence on the person who caused harm making it harder to name, let alone take action when the fear of financial stability is in play.

Sometimes the harm comes from an elderly grandparent, now frail, whom the family expects us to care for. In other cases, the person who caused harm is an in-law, and we find ourselves outnumbered by their family, who pressure us to "get over it," casting the offender as misunderstood or already forgiven. In these tangled distortions, the person calling for accountability often becomes the problem in the eyes of others.

The family dynamics are no easier to navigate once the authorities are involved. When someone is arrested or imprisoned for their actions, the outside world often assumes that justice has been done and the story is over. It rarely feels that way to those inside the family. Loving someone who has caused this kind of harm is disorienting, and yet love doesn't just disappear because these facts have surfaced. When the offending person is released, as most eventually are, the story continues.

As non-offending parents, our first and most urgent responsibility is ensuring the safety of all children. We cannot rely on promises alone. It is not enough to tell someone who has caused sexual harm to children, "Don't do it again." There must be sustained therapeutic support, and in many cases, serious and lasting restrictions on access to children.

Supervision and treatment are not interchangeable. Incarceration may temporarily remove access to potential victims, but it is not a path to healing. Even someone earnestly seeking recovery must not be placed in positions that ask others to take unnecessary risks. We must err on the side of caution and never confuse love with blind trust. Nor imagine the problem is solved because someone has lost their freedom.

These responsibilities can place non-offending parents in impossible positions. Where does a partner go if they cannot be left alone with children? What if we depend on an offending parent or grandparent for child care while we work? What happens when the breadwinner is jailed, and we are left alone to support the family? When there is not enough evidence to convict, does this person return home to life as it was? And then what? Not convicted is not the same as not guilty.

For many, we are holding the competing feelings of love and rage. It is possible to feel grief, anger, compassion, and care all at once. However, we must not confuse this with silence or complicity. We do not brush harm under the rug and call it a "mistake," hoping time will do the work for us.

We must stay present for our children's healing, no matter what happens to the person who caused the harm. That includes refusing to force the child who was harmed—whether they are five or fifty—to participate in family gatherings while the rest pretend nothing happened, or that it isn't as big of a deal as the non-offending parent is making it.

The responsibility remains. We are called to protect, to believe, to tell the truth, and to walk the long and uncertain path of healing with our children. That work often begins, as it did for Agnes, by allowing reality into the room. We can love them, see the reasons they may have arrived at this devastating behavior, all while making space for the impact on our child. We can not cancel out the wrong with what they did right. They must coexist.

Conclusion

For the non-offending parent, the path of healing is layered and demanding, marked by waves of conflicting emotions, painful truths, and the longing for clarity where none exists. This role calls for the strength to hold opposing feelings without being overtaken by any one of them, and the courage to stay present without rushing toward easy answers.

The ORANGE can become a source of quiet leadership rooted in compassion, integrity, and deep commitment to the family. We learn to forgive ourselves in moments of grace, to recognize small but meaningful shifts, and to trust that each act of clarity and care helps shape a safer future for the generations to come.

We cannot force change or heal in someone else's place, but we can take responsibility for our own boundaries and learning. We can help create a family culture where truth is spoken, harm is named, and repair is possible.

Making Space for Each Other

To **GREEN**, **BLUE** and **PURPLE**: In families impacted by sexual harm, everyone is hurting. While we may hope the ORANGE will show up emotionally balanced and clear about what's needed, the reality is that most people are unprepared to navigate this kind of harm.

We cannot expect them to say or do exactly what we need. They are also carrying the weight of their own inner world. Often, they simply don't know what to do or how to do it. This can be frustrating, disappointing and even hurtful, but the more we demand what feels obvious to us, the more they lose hope of ever getting it right. Eventually, under that pressure, ORANGES may stop trying or retreat altogether.

This doesn't mean excusing harmful behavior or abandoning our needs. It means recognizing that no one instinctively knows how to respond to sexual harm within a family system. When we make space for each other's imperfection, we keep the door open for growth, for accountability, and for real connection. Each person must find their own way forward. And while boundaries are often necessary, grace is just as vital.

CHAPTER 19

The Purple Experience

Purple: : Individuals who have caused sexual harm to a young person, who are no longer at risk of offending, and are ready to take responsibility as part of the healing.

For those who meet the definition above, know you are most welcome here. There is an important place at the table for those who have caused sexual harm to a young person and are ready to take responsibility.

When harm remains hidden, it splits our inner world. The secret we carry is not only harmful to the person we hurt, it is also corrosive to us. We may move through life with a quiet fear that someone will find out. In the case of sexual harm, we worry that if we take responsibility, it will be the only thing people ever see. That fear can shape our relationships, our sense of self, and our hope for the future.

Shame is not only carried by the person who was harmed; it is also borne heavily by the one who caused harm. Our coping mechanisms are often the same. We deny what happened, even to ourselves. We blame others or justify our behavior with experiences we have had. We minimize the impact on not just the victim but on others in our lives. We convince ourselves, through all kinds of distortions, that it wasn't harmful at all, that it was mutual or misunderstood.

And, just like everyone else in the family system, when we are ready to face the shame event and our part in it, we will begin to heal. We, too, must do our inner work in order to stand on solid ground and take part in the repair. This chapter is here to guide those who have caused sexual harm to see the path, not just forward, but through. Not one of erasure or punishment, but of reckoning, accountability, and the possibility of becoming someone who can help make healing possible for others, and for themselves.

Accountability as the Foundation of Healing

For those of us on the PURPLE path, healing begins with accountability. Without it, there is no foundation for growth, no way to rebuild trust, and no true path forward for ourselves or for those we've harmed. Accountability is not a one-time admission. It is an ongoing commitment to honesty, self-reflection, and meaningful change. It begins when we take full and unconditional ownership of the harm we have caused, without asking for forgiveness or understanding in return. We acknowledge, with clarity and humility: *I did that, and it was wrong.*

Accountability means recognizing that we do not get to shape the story of how our actions affected others. The impact belongs to the person who was harmed, not to us. Our role is not to explain it away, soften the blow, or insist that our intentions matter more than the outcome. True accountability invites us to meet the reality of what happened without defensiveness, without justification, and without delay.

This also means setting aside the stories we've told ourselves to lessen our responsibility. Some of these narratives may contain elements of truth, such as, "I was being sexually harmed too," or "I didn't understand the long-term impact on my brother's well-being." Others are outright falsehoods, like, "My stepdaughter seduced me," or "It was mutual and therefore not abuse." Whether partially true or completely distorted, these stories do not serve accountability. They may explain how we got there, but they do not excuse what we did. Healing cannot coexist with a justification of harm, not even when there were extenuating circumstances.

And yet, it is no surprise that we instinctively move away from accountability, especially when we have caused serious harm. Facing what we have done can feel unbearable. Shame, fear, and self-loathing can tempt us to retreat into silence or denial. We may think that by pretending it never happened, we are protecting others from more pain. In truth, we are protecting ourselves from the discomfort of being seen as less-than. We do not want to be misunderstood as only a person who caused sexual harm. It is understandable and we are avoiding the very thing that might allow us to begin healing.

To truly engage in accountability, we must build the strength and stamina to stay present with the discomfort. This means understanding the deeper reasons behind our actions and doing the internal work of coming to terms with ourselves. We begin to see the person we were, the person we are now, and the person we hope to become. Over time, with support and practice, we learn to hold the full weight of what we've done without turning away. This is not a performance. It is a slow, steady transformation rooted in truth, integrity, and humility.

Accountability is not easy, but it is possible. When we hold onto our intrinsic worth we are far more able to take responsibility for our actions, not only for those we harmed, but for ourselves as well.

Living With The Responsibility

Taking responsibility means more than acknowledging what we did in the past. It also requires us to stay attuned to how our presence impacts others now. Even when we are no longer causing direct harm, simply being known as someone who has caused sexual harm can bring fear, confusion, or pain to those around us. Accountability asks us to remain sensitive to that, to hold awareness of others' responses without defensiveness, and to respond with humility and care.

There is no finish line on this path. Accountability is not something we complete. It is something we carry. We continue to show up with honesty, adjusting our role as needed, and accepting that forgiveness or reconciliation may never come. We do not demand to be let back in. We rebuild a life where we can live in integrity, supported by those who love us and are willing to walk beside us on this journey.

While we are more than the harm we caused, we do not use that truth to sidestep the pain we inflicted. Instead, we let it ground us in the strength needed to face shame and turn it into meaningful repair. This work is not punishment. It is a chance to become someone worthy of trust. Not in words, but in our everyday actions.

For Those Not Yet Ready

If you are not yet prepared to confront past harmful actions or are struggling with harmful impulses, seek professional help immediately. Compassionate professionals and nonjudgmental communities exist to support you. Recovery and change are possible, but they require a willingness to engage.If you are reading this at someone else's insistence and feel resistance, consider setting the book aside. Return to it only when you feel genuine curiosity about how the information might apply to your life. This work must be voluntary to be effective.

Apologies and Amends

Apologies only land when they are rooted in genuine remorse. They cannot be demanded, scheduled, or offered to satisfy a sense of duty or guilt. Apologies that are forced, whether as part of a consequence or as a way to smooth things over, often deepen the wound. The only apology that carries meaning is one chosen freely, offered from a place of deep reflection and heartfelt regret. We must not fall into the trap of imagining an apology can heal simply because it has been spoken. Timing, sincerity, and self-awareness matter.

Remorse is not about talking. It is about listening, truly listening with empathy. When we sit with the reality of what we have done and allow ourselves to feel the pain we caused in someone else's body, mind, relationships, and self-worth, we begin to hurt *with* them. That is remorse. Often, we are not in a position to hear directly from the person we harmed. If they choose to speak with us, we must be ready to listen—not to defend, explain, or be forgiven—but to witness.

Amends are not gestures we invent to feel we are doing something to make up for the harm. They are not gifts, apologies, or money handed over in hopes of resolution. When offered from that place, they risk being seen as transactional, even as "blood money." Amends must come through a building relationship. They are not about what we think would help, but about what the person we harmed says they need, if and when they are ready to share it. That can only happen if we are willing to walk beside them without our own agenda.

There may be times when amends are not accepted, or when the person we harmed does not want to engage. We honor that choice without bitterness. We continue the work of accountability not to be let back in, but to live our own life with integrity. Through our actions over time, we show that healing and repair are possible, even if reconciliation never comes. This work is never about restoring our image. It is about restoring our humanity, one grounded in truth, humility, and the possibility of becoming someone who contributes to the safety and healing of others.

A Purple Story: *Harming a Loved One*

Manuel was only 9 when his friend Jeff introduced him to a dark world. Jeff's father would call the boys into his bedroom to watch pornography, teaching them to masturbate, speaking degradingly about the women on screen. This toxic environment warped Manuel's understanding of sexuality, power, respect for others and consent at a very young age.

At 11, he began sexually abusing his little sister, Abigail, who was six. She tried twice to tell her parents that she didn't want Manuel in her room at night. They dismissed this as normal sibling conflict not ever imagining what could be happening. She did not have the words or understanding herself to explain.

As she grew older, she became more vocal about not wanting him in her room, and asked for a lock for her bedroom door. Her parents grew concerned and started asking more questions and Manuel overheard them talking about sending her to therapy. Afraid of potential consequences, he stopped coming to her room and found other outlets for his sexual behavior.

As Manuel grew older, he began to comprehend the seriousness of what he had done. He felt a deep sense of shame that turned into rage toward his sister at times that seemingly came out of nowhere.

Confused and hurt by her brother's moody behavior, Abigail would shut down, turn inward, and wonder if she had done something wrong. She had blocked out the sexual harm years before.

Their parents thought it was sad when they didn't

get along, but assumed it was normal for siblings to be this way. Still, other times they got along well, and enjoyed each other. This was her big brother and she loved him. She appreciated it when he paid attention to her in a kind way. When he left for college she went into a deep depression.

Abigail began drinking, smoking and engaging in sex with people who were not respectful. She often woke up on Monday morning with feelings of self hate, not wanting to go to school to face the taunts from the boys, and the sneers from the girls. Rejection triggered suicidal thoughts, and the isolation from a lack of any true friendships made it worse.

College brought some improvement. She had always been smart and capable, despite everything else. She got out of her community and had a chance to start over. Abigail's drinking became more manageable, though it still surfaced during times of stress. She graduated with honors, her family bursting with pride, especially Manuel. It seemed Abigail was on the path to success.

The start of her adult life was rocky. She twice lost jobs because of migraines that made her unable to work for days. She searched for longer periods of time for work, but the promising jobs kept slipping away, crushing her spirits. Her parents tried to reassure her that another would come along but she pushed them away with her own wall of anger.

In therapy, Abigail uncovered memories of the sexual abuse she was subjected to by her older brother. It took years for her to unpack the memories, and the pain. She did so without letting her family know. She started to get better and her migraines subsided. She found a job and moved out of her parent's home.

With newfound agency and courage, she decided to confront Manuel and their parents. She wanted to tell Manuel she remembered what had happened. To her parents, she wanted to remind them of how she tried to get their help, and express her anger for not believing her when she was bravely speaking up. She sat them down, and when she finished talking she looked up to the impact of her words.

Her parents seemed shocked and struggling with disbelief. They were having a hard time integrating what was being said. They just looked at her with confusion, looking at each other and then back at her. They started to ask if this was a dream she had, or some kind of joke, when her brother, who had been silently looking down until then, burst forth with the truth.

His parents reacted badly, insisting to him it wasn't true, and trying to defend him to his sister. They kept saying they were sure everyone was remembering something else. They are sure they would have known if something like that was happening. This only made Manuel angry and he started screaming at them, blaming them for not protecting his sister while he sobbed with shame.

Abigail just stared at them, completely numb.

Relational Repair Within Families

When sexual harm has occurred within a family, the aftermath is rarely simple. Even when there is distance or silence, deep emotional bonds often remain. Love, guilt, confusion, longing, and anger can coexist in complicated and painful ways. For some survivors, there may be a desire to reconnect mixed with a need to maintain strong boundaries. For those who caused harm, there may be shame, regret, or uncertainty about whether and how to engage again. These tensions require enormous sensitivity and respect for each person's timing, needs, and emotional safety.

In families where the PURPLE is doing meaningful accountability work, it may be possible to rebuild a new way of relating, slowly, over time. This begins with consistency, humility, and a deep commitment to safety. When we acknowledge our actions without defensiveness and remain open to the truth of the pain we've caused, we create the possibility—though never the guarantee—of repair. When both people are ready, a new kind of relationship can form. One that doesn't erase what happened, but holds it with honesty, respect, and care.

Healing inside a family requires everyone involved to do their own work. Parents, siblings, and extended family members may all be affected, even if they weren't directly involved. When one person steps forward to disclose harm or take responsibility, it disrupts the existing narrative. Everyone must adjust to this new truth, and that can take time. For some, it may take years. There is no set script for what comes next, only a shared need for space, compassion, and emotional integrity.

Boundaries, Readiness, and Our Role

Even as we pursue accountability, we must remain grounded in the reality that not everyone will want or be ready to engage with us. Being part of a family system does not entitle us to restoration or reconciliation. Instead, we approach others with humility, aware that any invitation to participate in healing is just that—an invitation, not a given. When the person we harmed chooses to remain distant, we respect that choice without bitterness. Their agency and boundaries must remain intact, apart from anything else.

At the same time, we also attend to our own well-being. Walking the PURPLE path means holding ourselves accountable without collapsing under shame, less worth or accepting mistreatment. Accountability is not the same as enduring endless blame, aggressive treatment or accepting we must forego our own care. Boundaries are part of healing for everyone, including us. We do not seek to protect ourselves from responsibility, but we also do not abandon our right to safety, support, and a life of integrity.

If and when we are invited into connection, we treat that opportunity with reverence. It is not a moment to justify or to be forgiven, but a chance to bear witness to the pain we caused. We meet that pain with presence, not performance. Repair, if it comes, is slow and fragile. And even when it doesn't come, we continue this work. Not for reward or approval, but because it is the most honest way forward to our own healing.

A Turning Point

For families impacted by sexual harm, a disclosure can feel like the moment everything falls apart. It can also be the moment everything has a chance to change. In Manuel's family, Abigail's disclosure was the opening of a door.

Until that moment, they were all stuck: Manuel in denial, the parents in confusion, and Abigail carrying the burden into her daily life alone. Her courage gave the entire family the chance to see what had previously been obscured. It was not a gift she owed anyone, but an invitation of movement.

For Manuel, this moment could become a turning point. He was offered the chance to come into relationship with his family and the harm he had caused. The PURPLE path begins when we recognize these moments for what they are: rare and sacred opportunities to step out of our inauthentic self which has been burying the harm for too long, and into the open.

Many feel relieved when the secret is out, and everyone knows. There is no more hiding and the time to do the work is here. It is a privilege to be offered that chance, even if it arrives wrapped in pain. What we do with it is up to us.

Key Principles of the Purple Path

- **Center the Needs of Those Harmed:** Ask what they need from us now, and prioritize their needs above our own comfort.
- **Avoid Justifying or Minimizing:** When listening to the impact our behavior had on others, it is not the time to explain the why behind our actions. Focus on listening and not challenging the subjective truth of the speaker.
- **Accept the Role of Time:** Healing is a process that unfolds at its own pace. Be present to the rhythm of each person, and let go of controlling the process or hurrying it along our own preferred timeline.
- **Take Time to Develop Empathy:** Through deep inner work, we build the capacity to hold space for others' pain without defensiveness or distraction.
- **Offer Genuine Amends:** Amends are not transactions; they are sustained, meaningful actions that reflect the relationship to the one we harmed, our remorse and commitment to repair.
- **Seek Support:** The Purple Path is never walked alone. We need loved ones and authentic relationships to do this work. Connect with others on this journey to find strength and guidance.
- **Pace Yourself and Practice Self-Care:** This work is demanding. Prioritize our well-being to sustain the immense effort this takes. It is a marathon, not a sprint.

- **Let People Go If Needed:** Some may distance themselves, temporarily or permanently. Respect their boundaries, process the grief associated with the loss, and continue the work; they may find their way back if it is meant to be.

This path is long and nonlinear, requiring patience, humility, and a deep understanding that true repair comes through consistent, intentional effort over time. The work is not about achieving a final resolution but about choosing, every day, to be someone who adds light to the world, no matter how far we have come or how much further there is to go.

The Complexity of Young Adult Sexual Harm

Young adulthood is a pivotal stage of sexual development, where individuals are still cultivating maturity, relational skills, and a full understanding of consent. At this age, the part of the brain responsible for impulse control, long-term planning, and evaluating consequences remains in development. This biological reality influences decision-making and can limit a young person's ability to fully grasp the consequences of their actions. The encouraging news is that, with appropriate guidance, education, and accountability, most young adults can learn and adopt healthier behaviors.

While inexperience plays a significant role, it is only part of the picture. Young adults are also shaped by cultural norms, peer dynamics, exposure to pornography, and the influence of mood-altering substances. These factors can distort understanding, impair judgment, and contribute to harmful behavior, especially in sexual situations where power, pressure, or emotional intensity are involved.

Pornography, in particular, distorts perceptions of intimacy, consent, and honoring boundaries, often portraying coercive behaviors or forced encounters as acceptable or even desirable. Combined with substance use, peer pressure, and a lack of relational experience, these influences can contribute to poor choices and miscommunication that lead to harmful sexual encounters.

Acknowledging these complexities is not about diminishing the experience of those who were harmed. Sexual harm is always serious and has lasting consequences for the person impacted, regardless of the intentions or developmental stage of the one who caused it. The purpose here is to explore the factors that contribute to sexual harm from the perspective of young adults who perpetrate it—not to excuse their actions, but to better understand them. This nuanced perspective allows us to craft interventions that address root causes and equip young adults with the skills needed to navigate intimate relationships responsibly.

Consider the following:

1. Inexperience and Misunderstanding

Many young adults enter sexual relationships or encounters without the communication skills or knowledge needed to navigate them effectively. In these instances, harm stems from inexperience or misunderstanding rather than malicious intent. A young person might, for example, misinterpret silence as consent or struggle to respond appropriately when something changes during a sexual interaction.

When they later realize their actions caused harm, they often feel deeply ashamed, genuinely confused and desperate to make it right with the other person. These individuals would never have intentionally caused harm, especially in such a personal and significant way.

This type of harm calls for a response centered on education and opportunities for repair. Supported conversations where the individual who caused harm listens to the impact of their actions, gains nuanced understanding of what they could have done differently, and offers genuine apologies can be far more effective in meeting the needs of the one harmed. These restorative approaches often provide more lasting outcomes than formal or punitive processes, especially when intent to harm is absent and the person who caused harm is willing to learn.

Formal legal processes are normally not the right approach in these situations. Too often, our systems respond with punishment even in situations where the evidence is lacking and the harm was clearly unintentional. This can leave the person who was harmed without true acknowledgment of their experience, and the person who caused harm without the tools or insight needed to do better. Worse still, it may discourage genuine remorse by teaching young people to defend themselves rather than reflect, apologize, and work toward repair.

When young people are met with clarity, guidance, and accountability, rather than shame or labels, they are more likely to internalize the lessons and be open to remorse. They develop the capacity to become communicative, respectful, and have a more nuanced awareness of consent. This approach not only supports those directly involved, but also contributes to the prevention of future harm.

It is important to distinguish between harm caused through inexperience and harm that is deliberate or coercive. Treating all instances of sexual harm as the same can alienate those who would otherwise be willing to take responsibility, learn, and make amends. It may also distort the path of healing for the person who was harmed, leaving them entangled in a process that prioritizes punishment over understanding. When adults step in with clarity and care, we can offer better guidance, and support both accountability and healing.

2. Coercion and Emotional Force

Some young adults, shaped by societal dysfunction, pornography, and unhealthy role models, develop ingrained misconceptions about their own entitlement in sexual relationships or encounters. These beliefs can manifest as coercive behaviors such as guilt inducing pressure, persistence even after being told no, and emotional manipulation until the other gives in rather than freely consents.

This can also include ignoring a partner's change of mind during an encounter or treating consent as a one-time, irreversible transaction. While physical force may be absent, the emotional pressure used to override a partner's autonomy is deeply damaging, leaving those on the receiving end feeling violated, ashamed, and disconnected from their sense of agency.

These behaviors indicate a distorted understanding of sexual relationships and an immaturity that may derive from inexperience and sexual insecurity. They may believe that "getting" sex is the goal, and persistence proves desire. These ideas are reinforced by peers, media, and inadequate education, reflecting a larger societal failure to equip young people with the tools for healthy intimacy.

Addressing these behaviors requires more than condemnation; it demands intentional, constructive intervention to break through the focus on self-interest only. Young adults in this category benefit from structured opportunities for growth through education, peer support, and professional guidance. Response programs can teach empathy, relational skills, and the principles of consent, challenging harmful misconceptions and fostering respect for boundaries.

This process includes natural consequences, such as the loss of trust, exclusion from social settings or strained relationships, but isolating or shaming someone who is willing to learn may do more harm than good. When we surround young people with peers, mentors, and educators who model accountability and respectful behavior, we help them find a different way to relate to potential intimate partners.

These young adults are not beyond reach. With compassionate, honest guidance from adults, they can begin to unlearn harmful beliefs and build relationships that honor both their own needs and the autonomy of others. This is not just about individual change. It is about creating a culture of consent, empathy, and mutual respect that reduces harmful encounters and strengthens intimate relationships for all young people.

3. Intentional Harm

The most serious category of sexual abuse among young adults involves knowingly and intentionally harming others sexually. This includes taking advantage of someone who is incapacitated, ignoring clearly stated boundaries, or continuing despite visible signs of distress.

When these behaviors are premeditated—such as deliberately administering a substance like Rohypnol to an unknowing victim to limit their ability to resist, or luring someone into a vulnerable situation in order to use force—the urgency for intervention becomes even greater. These actions reflect a profound disregard for another person's well-being and call for immediate, structured containment. Without appropriate response, these patterns are likely to persist.

While this level of harm may seem beyond repair, it is essential to remember that young people are still in the process of developing. The parts of the brain responsible for impulse control, empathy, and long-term decision-making are not yet fully mature. This creates a critical window of opportunity. Early intervention, grounded in structure, support, and accountability, can interrupt patterns before they become deeply entrenched.

This is not to excuse the seriousness of the harm or minimize its impact on the victim. Those who have been harmed in this intentional way deserve immediate protection, validation from the adults around them, and access to every available resource to support their healing. The trauma they carry may be lifelong, and the seriousness of the violation must be fully acknowledged.

At the same time, intervening with a young person who has caused intentional harm offers a unique opportunity—one that may not be as accessible later in life. Young adults who engage in this behavior often lack empathy, insight, or the emotional tools needed to regulate themselves. With consistent, long-term treatment, however, many can begin the process of unlearning harmful sexual behavior and entering into recovery.

Recovery-focused interventions provide a more constructive path than punishment alone. These programs help young people examine the roots of their behavior, take responsibility for the harm they've caused, and learn how to build respectful, non-coercive relationships. Structured environments that limit access to others while offering space for deep internal work can protect potential victims while supporting the possibility of real change.

With time, consistency, and accountability, some young people may become capable of rejoining their families and communities in safe, grounded, and relational ways. Investing in recovery over retribution does not excuse the behavior. It increases the chances that the harm will not be repeated. It offers a path toward transformation, one that holds safety, accountability, and the possibility of becoming someone new.

A Culture Beyond Cancellation

When accusations of sexual harm surface, our first reaction often comes fast and strong. Cancel culture feeds on this immediacy—driven by pain, outrage, and the urge to take a side. Rushing to conclusions without all the information rarely helps and often makes it worse. Feelings are not facts, and outside of a courtroom, none of us are responsible for determining guilt.

What we *are* responsible for is slowing down, holding space for the nuance, the complexity, and responding with discernment. Believing and supporting the person who feels sexually harmed does not require publicly condemning the one accused. We can honor the survivor's experience *and* allow space to understand what happened more fully before leaping to take a side. There are no sides in sexual harm, just a dearth of those willing to support the healing and accountability.

When someone we care about is accused of sexual harm, the most meaningful thing we can do is stay in connection. Not to accuse, and not to excuse, but to offer a steady, nonjudgmental presence as they begin to work through what happened. Denial, minimization, and blaming others are common responses to shame. This is only the starting point.

When we are able to hold space for their full humanity and remain open to supporting their accountability, something important can happen. That same person may begin to reflect, recognize where they crossed a line, and name what they regret. When people believe they must either defend themselves or lose everything, they will shut down the very conditions that make taking responsibility possible.

Learning to pause, to withhold judgment, and to stay in relationship with those who are willing to grow is how we shift this culture of harm. We move from silence and division toward peer support, adult guidance, and real accountability. We get to fewer acts of sexual harm by creating a climate where responsibility is possible and expected, not punishing someone into hiding.

Building a better culture doesn't mean excusing harm. It means responding in a way that supports healing, accountability, and change. It means believing that young people can learn and evolve. And it means offering the kind of compassion that keeps doors open, not just for justice, but for transformation.

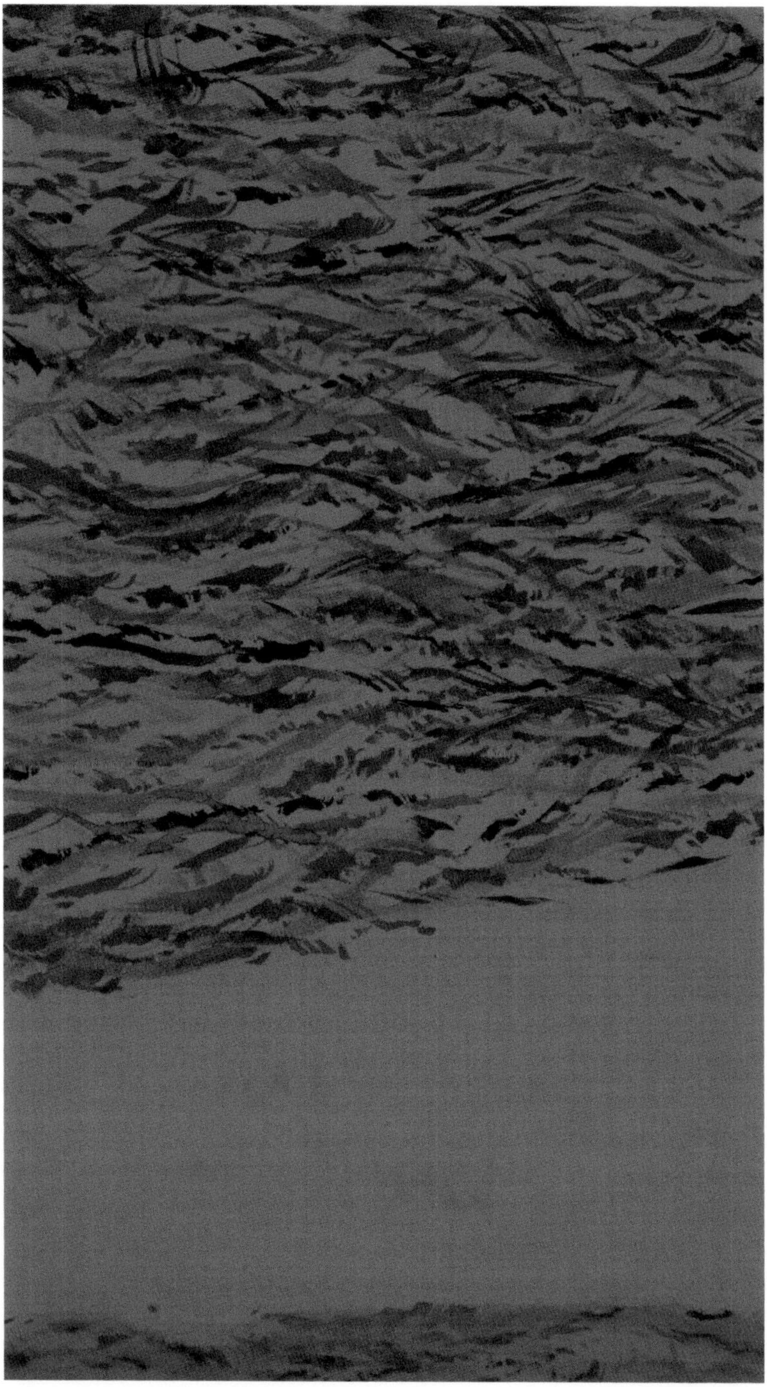

PART V

CHAPTER 20

Waves of Family Harm

For too long, we've labored under the misguided belief that sexual abuse affects only the victim, leaving them solely responsible for their healing while the rest of us stand by as passive observers to their struggle. We've extended invitations to family gatherings, perplexed by the deteriorating connection, and gradually lost hope in our GREEN's ability to cross an imaginary finish line of recovery.

When we broaden our perspective and recognize sexual harm as a trauma that reverberates through the entire family system, strange as it seems, there is more hope because there is more power for each individual to alter the dynamic. This shift in understanding empowers each family member to take on part of the pain, and take on part of the responsibility for recovery, lessening it for everyone else.

Most families lack both the structural framework and the necessary knowledge to respond effectively to sexual harm. Instead of acting as a cohesive unit, individual family members often react based on their own emotional experiences, temperament and assumptions about how to move forward. These reactions are frequently driven by feelings, not logic.

As a result, each person may focus on their own perceived needs or ideas about what should happen next, creating a patchwork of responses that are uncoordinated and, at times, contradictory. This lack of alignment can unintentionally amplify instability within the family system and make it more challenging to address the harm constructively.

This pattern of disjointed responses often continues until someone steps up to take a leadership role. Ideally, this isn't the person who experienced the harm. Expecting them to both heal and educate the family places an unfair and often painful burden on them, especially when the family's confusion or resistance deepens their sense of being misunderstood or unsupported. When someone else takes on this leadership role, they can help guide the family toward a more intentional and collaborative path forward.

Child sexual abuse impacts systems rather than an isolated individual. It extends in concentric circles beyond the individual, permeating family relationships, community connections, and broader social systems. This manifests both through the direct consequences of the original harm but also through the reactions, actions, and inactions of others. This aspect of the system impact can create ongoing harm that is rarely acknowledged. These patterns, often unconscious, become part of the aftermath of the abuse.

The phenomenon of intergenerational child sexual abuse underscores this systemic dynamic. When past violations remain undisclosed, unaddressed, or unhealed the resulting silence and unresolved pain weaken a family's protective boundaries. This lack of acknowledgment and healing creates conditions where further harm can more easily occur.

Acknowledging the interconnected nature of sexual abuse in a family offers a path forward. Recognizing that the responsibility for recovery does not rest solely with the survivor but is a shared endeavor for the entire family. This collective commitment not only supports the survivor but also strengthens the family as a whole, building resilience and reducing the likelihood of further harm.

The following story explores how family dynamics play a role in perpetuating or addressing cycles of abuse. It illustrates how silence and avoidance can extend pain but also how courage and honest communication can pave the way for change. It invites us to examine our own roles within our families and the power we each have to contribute to a healthier future.

A Family Story: *Intergenerational Sexual Harm*

Alice and her older brother Thomas raised their daughters, Gabriella and Rose, in the same close-knit neighborhood they grew up in. Now in their forties, these sister-like-cousins were raising their own children in the same neighborhood, continuing the tradition of familial closeness.

One balmy evening, Gabriella and Rose sat with their husbands engaging in their weekly card game, laughing and drinking wine. Gabriella regaled them with a humorous anecdote about her uncle Thomas - Rose's father. The mood suddenly shifted dramatically when Rose's husband, his face contorted with anger, stood up and shouted, "Your uncle is a pedophile!" before storming out, leaving a stunned silence in his wake.

Rose did not expect her husband to reveal her abuse that evening, in that way. He later apologized but explained he couldn't pretend anymore, and it was past time to tell Gabriella. Over the next month, Gabriella and Rose engaged in painful, revealing conversations about how Rose's father had harmed her on a regular basis while her mother was out of town.

The cousins had always been close. Gabriella could

not believe she had no idea this had been going on. In support and solidarity, she accompanied Rose to her therapy sessions, their united front gave Rose courage. She reached a point when she felt ready to disclose this to Gabriella's mother - Thomas' sister - to get some support in speaking with her own parents.

When they approached Alice one afternoon when she was alone in the house, asking if they could speak to her about something painful, she sat down looking afraid. Before they spoke a word, Alice blurted out "I know what you are going to say." The cousins looked at each other with confusion. Alice offered, "It happened to me too. My brother, Thomas. I know how he is. Let's just say he has always had a hard time keeping it in his pants."

She started to weep. Rose and Gabriella said nothing. She ended her long cry and the conversation they had started, thanking them for listening and soothing her. Then she got up to leave, saying, "Well, that is all in the past now. My advice, Rose, is to enjoy the good things in life and try not to think about it too much." She quickly left the room leaving her daughter and niece to process without her.

In the aftermath of this conversation, an icy chill descended upon the once-warm extended family. Rose felt betrayed by her aunt. She wondered if she had been in a position to prevent the harm but did not. When Rose had found the courage to talk to her about it, she had ended up on the listening end of her aunt's pain. Alice had shown no empathy for her, nor much to say except the unhelpful advice of "try not to think about it too much."

Alice started to suffer from an intense depression after that, unwilling to grapple with her own resurfacing trauma. Her husband was very much in the dark about what was happening but he stayed silent about it, and didn't ask. His typical MO when it came to his wife and daughter. Gabriella encouraged her mother to see a therapist, or at least tell her dad what happened. Alice began declining invitations from her sister-in-law, and distanced herself from her brother's home. She canceled family traditions. Tellingly, no one said a word about it or questioned why.

Alice avoided Gabriella. If she brought up the topic again, Alice wasn't sure she would be able to recover from another conversation. Gabriella tried to talk to Rose about her mother's decline. This resulted in Rose getting angry at Gabriella for once again expecting her to hold the feelings of her aunt's while no one was holding hers. Their husbands tried to mend the fences but it was too raw for everyone.

A year passed with no momentum toward healing. It was as if the whole family fell into a dreamstate. The older generation was unwilling to open Pandora's box. The younger generation of adults grieving the loss of their closest support network but not sure how to move past what had transpired. They were all stuck.

One day, Rose's daughter saw an invitation on the counter to join her grandfather's 80th birthday party. She wanted to go. Her mom, ill-equipped to explain the situation to the children, felt she had little choice. Rose called Gabriella for help.

Gabriella sat down with her cousin to figure out the best step forward. To her credit, she offered to do whatever Rose needed, including confront their parents about what had happened. Rose was not ready for that, but asked if they could all go to the party together, and stick together.

With some encouragement from her husband, Alice also agreed to go to the party. She was hoping that it would break the ice that had formed between all of them. She was confident that at a party, no one would raise the past or confront the issue, and if they did, she was going to walk right out the front door.

The invitation carried the weight of a year's worth of silence and generations of pain. It was clear that the grandmothers, in their desire for normalcy, were attempting to paper over the cracks in their family's foundation with no intention of addressing the source of the damage.

As the day of the gathering approached, tension mixed with anticipation. Gabriella, Rose and their husbands sat together before this birthday dinner sharing their feelings with one another. They vowed to stick together through this event, and have Rose's back, whatever was necessary. They vowed to keep the children safe from sexual harm by staying vigilant, and work together to confront Thomas when the time was right.

This story, rather than providing a neat resolution, reveals a complicated chapter in this family's life. Their unaddressed trauma slows the pace for everyone as this difficult path toward recovery unfolds. It demonstrates the cost of silence, the bravery and emotional support required to face painful truths, and the delicate balance between maintaining family bonds and addressing deeply rooted wounds. As with this family, it cannot be resolved in a single conversation, or action.

In the aftermath of disclosure, four distinct waves of harm often unfold within a family system. While I present these waves in a linear sequence for simplicity, the reality is far more nuanced. My hope is that these general patterns can serve as a framework to help us better understand

and navigate the pivotal relational moments within our own families.

The wave of harm we are most familiar with—the one we desperately wish we could have prevented—is the harm itself. This initial wave occurs when someone exploits a power imbalance to sexually gratify themselves at the expense of a young person.

This act forms The First Wave of Harm.

The First Wave of Harm begins with the abuse itself but is not limited to that event. It also includes the silence and secrecy that often surround it, whether imposed by the abuser, internalized by the victim, or maintained by the family. This silence can stretch on for years, delaying healing and compounding the original trauma. During this time, the person who was harmed may carry the burden of a secret or may have no conscious memory of the abuse, especially if it occurred in early childhood.

For many survivors, healing eventually brings a pivotal moment of disclosure. Often this comes in adulthood, when they've developed enough safety and self-awareness to name what happened. The path forward is shaped not only by the original harm but by how those around the survivor respond when the truth finally comes to light.

This brings us to The Second Wave of Harm.

Disclosing past sexual abuse to a loved one is a significant moment for a survivor. The naming of that experience out loud to a trusted witness is also an action step toward healing. When met with compassion, the listener can create a sense of solidarity, conveying, "You don't have to face this alone.

The Second Wave of Harm arises when the family member is unable to meet a disclosure with the emotional presence and grounded support that it requires. While the first wave is defined by the original abuse and the silence that follows, this second wave is shaped by the reactions of those who hear the truth. Disclosures are vulnerable, often hard-won moments, and the way they are received has the power either to begin repair or to deepen the wound.

It is not easy to hold a disclosure well. For many, hearing about child sexual abuse triggers a cascade of overwhelming emotions and fears: What does this mean for our family? What has to change? What am I supposed to do? I can't imagine this could happen in our family. Do I even believe this is possible? Maybe this was just a misunderstanding. This internal flood of reactions can make it hard to stay present and supportive to the survivor.

Cognitive dissonance can also get in the way. People often struggle to reconcile what they're hearing with who they believe the person who caused harm to be. That dissonance is magnified by the "ick factor"—a deep discomfort many feel when talking about sexual harm, especially when it involves children. And for some, like Alice, unprocessed personal histories of abuse can further disrupt their ability to respond with clarity and care. When our own trauma is still raw, someone else's disclosure can stir pain we're not prepared to face.

These internal reactions often lead to responses that don't help and sometimes cause real damage. Minimizing, denying, changing the subject, focusing on logistics, or centering one's own emotions instead of the person who was harmed can all weaken the healing potential of the moment.

In Alice's case, she used a disclosure of her own trauma to deflect accountability, leaving Rose without the support she needed. Rose's mother, faced with the unbearable reality of both her daughter's potential disclosure and her husband's actions, fell silent and withdrew, creating even more isolation for her child. This kind of retreat, even when it comes from confusion or pain, compounds the harm already done.

So what does a supportive response look like? In the moment, it doesn't require fixing anything or making decisions. It only requires presence. The most powerful thing you can do is listen with empathy.

Stay grounded. Acknowledge what's been shared without minimizing it. Sitting in the discomfort, without deflecting, justifying, or rushing to solutions, creates a space where the person who was harmed can begin to feel seen, believed, and safe. That alone is an act of profound support.

Still, when families are unable to hold that space, when reactions are shaped more by internal chaos than by care, the harm is ongoing. And when the opportunity for support is missed, it often sets the stage for the next inevitable familial response.

The Third Wave of Harm

The Third Wave of Harm begins when the initial crisis of disclosure becomes too uncomfortable to sustain. At first, emotions such as confusion, grief, anger, fear run high but without clear leadership or tools for resolving conflict, the family's energy for facing the harm eventually dissipates. Over time, the intensity fades, and an uneasy quiet settles in. Slowly, people stop talking about it. Life moves forward, in some ways, as if nothing had ever been disclosed.

This return to normalcy often includes resuming relationships or routines that feel insensitive or require the survivor to tolerate their own discomfort for the sake of the family. When family members reconnect with the person who caused the harm without also expecting them to take responsibility, work toward safety, or seek understanding, it can feel like a profound betrayal.

At first, disclosure can feel like a relief. Finally, the truth is out. When nothing changes, the relief can quickly give way to something far more devastating. For many survivors, it was one thing when the family didn't know. But once they do and still go on as if nothing happened, it lands as a deep, disorienting betrayal. Not just disappointment, but grief. The kind of grief that comes from realizing: *My well-being is not a priority.*

This dynamic is rarely driven by malice. More often, it stems from confusion, fear, or a lack of knowledge. Family members may feel overwhelmed by what healing requires, especially in a system without clear leadership. They may also be struggling with their own pain, like Alice, who accepted Thomas's birthday invitation in an effort to move forward. Or Rose's mother, who fell silent, perhaps to avoid confronting her husband's role in the abuse.

These responses are human. And still, they leave the survivor profoundly alone. Right when they most need to be seen, believed, and supported. In this atmosphere, the survivor is often left with an impossible choice: suppress their pain to stay connected to the family, or create distance in order to heal. Staying may offer a sense of belonging, but it often comes at the cost of self-abandonment. Leaving may offer the space needed for healing, but it can also mean walking away from the only support system they've ever known.

This third wave echoes the original abuse: *your needs matter less than satisfying the needs of others, regardless of the impact that might have on you*. When families pressure survivors to forgive quickly, minimize the harm, or "move on" for the sake of peace, they unintentionally reinforce this painful message.

And we arrive at The Final Wave.

The Final Wave of Harm brings the family full circle, as the system gravitates back to its pre-disclosure state. This collective attempt to metaphorically rebottle the shame event and erase the painful history from the family's shared awareness reflects a deeply rooted human desire for stability and equilibrium.

This return to 'normalcy' often manifests in ways that feel baffling to the one who was harmed. Funny family stories about the person who caused harm resurface without acknowledgment of their past actions, holiday gatherings proceed without regard for the survivor's emotional well-being, and major life events carry on as if the disclosure never happened.

From an outside perspective, such behavior may seem unfathomable.

Yet families often arrive at this point from exhaustion. Most people have no idea how to go about changing the culture of a family to support healing after abuse. Naturally the family members start to gravitate toward those who can give a reprieve from the heaviness of talking about the past abuse. It becomes unconsciously self-reinforcing. To be included, we must show up with lightness and keep quiet about the harm.

Maintaining this fragile sense of harmony often depends on unspoken agreements about who can stay comfortably inside the family's inner circle and who cannot. Over time, this can divide the family into those who are willing to uphold the peace, and those who are not. Survivors, in particular, may find they cannot hold both their healing and the family's emotional equilibrium at the same time. When they choose to speak honestly or set boundaries that disrupt the status quo, it can cause distress and conflict in the family. Rather than being seen as the one most affected by the harm, the survivor may begin to be perceived as the source of ongoing instability.

By insisting on talking about what happened, and how it is impacting them, the survivor can become the target of family frustration. When others struggle to confront their direct or indirect connection to the shame event, they may adopt an alternate narrative. This choice often prioritizes preserving the family's structure and functionality over jeopardizing valued family relationships.

This shift is not normally conscious or intentional. Often, it reflects the family's attempt to preserve the good they once had in the only way they know how. They often feel like they can not do anything right, and the survivor may blame them even when they try. The result is a painful reversal, where the one trying to heal is treated as the problem and pushed to the periphery, and a willingness to move on or go back to what once was becomes the condition for belonging.

Whether survivors choose to suppress their needs in order to remain connected to the family or step away to preserve their reality and work toward healing, the family system inevitably finds its way back to equilibrium. However, that balance often comes at a cost for both the survivor and the family. When a survivor stays, it may require silencing themselves and carrying their pain alone. This inevitably will lead to more long-term symptoms and conflict within the family system. When they leave, they all must face the grief of separation and the burden of being fractured as a family. In either case, the system stabilizes but not without harm, or not without loss.

Yet recognizing this pattern opens the door to another possibility. Families can learn to make time for both joy and lightness, and healing work. It is possible to build a family culture where vulnerability is met with compassion, where harm is acknowledged rather than hidden, and where the well-being of all is prioritized.

CHAPTER 21

Confining Archetypes

Like shifting weather patterns, our reactions within the family system naturally come and go with our emotional states. In the aftermath of sexual harm, family members often adopt ways of responding as the system struggles to regain balance. While we cannot control the emotions that arise or our immediate responses, we can prepare by understanding the strengths and limitations of some common sets of behaviors which we will call archetypes.

Our responses are, in part, shaped by personal histories, temperaments, family expectations, and access to resources. These archetypes can be positive in many ways, and when we use them at key moments, intentionally, they can benefit all. They also have their limitations. This chapter is an invitation to be conscious about how we are showing up at different times, and for what reasons. Remembering that emotional states are not permanent, and each day is a chance to start again.

By recognizing and understanding our responses, we empower ourselves to take actions aligned with our best selves. We may have said or done things in the past that we now regret. Responding well to harm is difficult, and many of us simply did not (or still do not) know how.

The good news is that repair is almost always possible. We can begin by acknowledging how we missed the moment to respond in a better way. We can ask the person what the impact was on them, and listen with empathy. We can express remorse, offer a sincere apology, and let them know we understand where we went wrong and are committed to doing better.

Healing is a dynamic interpersonal and intrapersonal process where opportunities for growth and self evolution are baked in. We can't expect ourselves to emerge fully equipped to support others in all the ways they need. We must make room to learn, make mistakes and be gracious about others when they stumble. No one can expand their perspective when they are being judged and criticized.

The depth of our personal inner work directly shapes our ability to navigate the emotional undercurrents of the family system. Those who have cultivated a sense of internalized safety, surrounded themselves with support, and committed to prioritizing self-care are often best positioned to take on leadership roles in the healing process. Building a family culture that respects boundaries and encourages open communication about difficult topics is essential. A key step toward meaningful change is identifying who within the family is ready to lead and who is willing to support that leadership.

Below, I've outlined several archetypal roles that family members often assume in the wake of sexual harm. These descriptions are not rigid labels but flexible frameworks designed to help us understand our own reactions and those of our loved ones. They provide a shared language for examining the complex dynamics that arise in families confronting the aftermath of sexual abuse.

I invite you to approach these roles with both caution and compassion. They are not intended to pigeonhole or judge individuals but to shed light on the various ways family members might respond to trauma. By understanding these roles, we can anticipate challenges, adapt our behaviors, and create more constructive interactions for the benefit of everyone involved.

As we explore these archetypes, remember they are tools for self-awareness and understanding, not accusations. Use this framework to recognize patterns, prepare for emotional "weather changes," and guide your family toward a more supportive and healing environment. With this shared vocabulary, we can work to prevent "role exhaustion" by recognizing that we do not need to always embody this archetype. We owe it to ourselves to foster a balanced, compassionate approach to this collective healing.

The Victim Advocate

If a family is fortunate, someone (other than the GREEN) will take on the role of an advocate. This individual, motivated by a strong commitment to supporting the survivor and preventing further harm, can drive meaningful change within the family system. Their dedication to addressing past wrongs and safeguarding future generations comes from a place of love, justice, and often their own pain.

The advocate often takes on the challenging task of confronting the person who caused harm, seeking some sense of accountability. They resist when the family starts to fall back into old patterns, routinely drawing fire from the others. They become a steadfast supporter of the survivor, sometimes at the cost of other relationships. Their commitment can be so absolute that they are often willing to "die on this hill" if necessary.

Advocates, while supportive in many ways, may experience their own secondary trauma. As they strive to align others with their perspective, they might face a collective push back that can be extremely stressful. Encounters with family members who minimize the harm or resist change can be stressful and, at times, retraumatizing.

The advocate's unwavering commitment to justice can lead to feelings of isolation, especially as others, sometimes even the survivor, attempt to return to familiar patterns. Over time, the advocate may feel as though they are carrying the responsibility for change alone, further compounding their sense of burden. It can be distressing to be the last one standing while the rest of the family system pushes back and treats the advocate as if they are the problem.

Advocates play a vital role in relieving the survivor from the constant need to defend or explain themselves. While this can bring support to the one who was harmed, advocates must also be mindful of their own well-being. Self-care and recognizing the limits of personal influence are required for sustaining this important role over the long haul.

One person alone cannot transform an entire family system. We can not force healing upon others, as human beings will naturally resist pressure, even if under different circumstances they may agree with the advocate. As we have been saying in past chapters, healing is a choice each individual must make for themselves. When two or more gather behind a gentle but firm advocacy position, it will create far more change with far less burden on the individuals than if one person takes up this mantle alone.

A small, united core within the family can act as a potent catalyst for change. This "family within a family" can mindfully establish new boundaries and live by them without pressuring others to see it differently. Picture a circle within a circle: the outer ring clings to old patterns, while the inner core, what we call 'the ball of light', operates with integrity, clarity, and compassion.

Don't waste energy trying to convince the outer circle to see it differently. Simply embody the change, and model it. As that light grows stronger, it will naturally draw others toward it. One day, this ball of light may take over the whole family. For now, it is enough to stand in our own integrity with confidence and shine from there a new way of being in the family.

Start by establishing the ground rules we want to live by. For example, we might decide not to attend family gatherings where the person who caused harm will be present, unless they have begun doing the work of repair. We may also set a boundary to check in with the person who was harmed before making decisions about hosting events or finalizing guest lists. We may determine that we will not get into conversations about the harm or the boundaries unless the other person is willing to also listen, and not demand compliance.

Advocates can lead by setting and maintaining personal boundaries, modeling healthy behavior, and refusing to participate in harmful dynamics. These actions often speak louder than words, showing others that there are more respectful ways to relate. When we hold our boundaries calmly and without judgment, without trying to push others to see it our way, or do as we do, we create a foundation for at least our relationships to reflect our values. Over time, this kind of steady modeling can inspire collective change.

By pacing ourselves and committing to the long game, advocates create space for family transformation. As they find allies and build momentum, their courage in speaking up and standing firm becomes the fuel for moving forward.

The Return to Normal.

Within many families, the journey toward a sense of normalcy often follows two distinct paths, shaped by differing needs and experiences.

The first path is taken by those who have been engaging with the pain, and have been offering steadfast support to others during the most difficult periods. These individuals may have been pillars of strength by answering late-night calls, providing comfort during moments of despair, and standing by their loved ones through intense challenges.

After prolonged immersion in this process, they often find themselves needing a reprieve. A chance to rest. They do not intend to step away entirely, only to prioritize their own well-being until they feel restored. Their desire for normalcy reflects a genuine need for a break in hopes of some renewal, enabling them to continue playing a supportive role.

The second path is often chosen by those who have more or less avoided confronting the pain. These family members may have distanced themselves emotionally, coping through denial or detachment. Their push for a "return to normal" stems from a desire to escape the discomfort, clinging to an idealized version of the past and hoping that silence or avoidance will restore the family's previous sense of order.

Both paths arise from human needs, but they have markedly different effects on the one who was harmed and the family system at large. Taking time for rest and renewal is healthy and necessary, but attempting to permanently revert to a pre-disclosure or pre-harm state is neither realistic nor supportive of recovery. The key lies in recognizing which path we (or others) are on and why, so we can navigate these dynamics with clarity and care.

When navigating these waters, several principles can guide us:

1. **Acknowledge Things Have Changed**
   As we navigate the instinct to reclaim what once was, it's important to acknowledge that things have fundamentally changed. Stating plainly that we know there is no returning to a previous time or way of being. And, our need for lightness is not an attempt to push things under the rug. We can acknowledge while the new normal may be challenging, it is not entirely negative. It can still be co-created, in some ways, upon the foundation of the good that existed before the harm.

2. **Practice Conscious Engagement**
   When encountering someone who is not yet ready to engage in the healing process but is pressuring others to "move on," it can be helpful to offer a compassionate reframe: "I understand that you're not ready to face this yet, and I recognize how difficult it can be. What do you think needs to shift for you to feel ready to see how things have changed since the harm event?" This approach acknowledges their current state with empathy while gently framing their reluctance within the broader context of the healing journey ahead.

If we recognize that we are the ones who are not yet emotionally prepared to confront the harm or the changes it brings, we can offer a version of this honesty to others: "I'm beginning to see that there's no easy way around this. I'm just not ready to face it yet. I need some time, and I ask for your patience while I figure it out." Sharing this openly reassures loved ones that we understand the larger context and the work ahead. It also allows us to move at our own pace without unintentionally causing harm to those around us.

3. **Holding Healthy Boundaries**

   The key to embodying the role of 'return to normalcy' effectively lies in remaining attuned to others' needs and emotional states while maintaining a clear sense of our own. We strive not to project our inner world onto others, nor to adopt theirs as our own. Instead, we can observe and hold space for what is happening within ourselves and others, allowing these experiences to coexist without merging or overshadowing one another.

   It is natural and healthy to seek moments of lightness and normalcy. However, we must take care not to inadvertently silence important conversations or dismiss the emotions of others. Assuming that everyone feels as we do or trying to persuade them to adopt our perspective risks undermining their unique process. By maintaining sensitivity and honoring diverse experiences, we create space for genuine connection and mutual understanding.

4. **Honor Self-Determination**

   When others encourage us to move forward before we feel ready, we have the right to set boundaries without guilt. If someone is pressuring us to rejoin social activities or revert to familiar patterns, we can simply say, "I am not ready for that yet, but thank you." Acknowledging their intent to include us while honoring our own need for more time can remind ourselves and others that we, as adults, have our own agency. Trusting our own pace is key to genuine healing.

Similarly, when others suggest how we should go about our healing, we maintain firm boundaries. As we have said, this process is deeply personal, and what works for one may not work for another. For any steps toward healing to be effective, they must be chosen freely. Recognizing these decisions as belonging to the individual helps prevent resentment from taking root.

We can always say, "Thank you for the suggestion. I can see how that might work for you or others, but it doesn't quite feel right for me at this time. I need to find my own way to heal from harm, but I do appreciate your intention to help. What would be supportive is..."

When we are trying to support others, it is equally important to respect their pace, their decisions and boundaries. Pushing someone into healing work that doesn't resonate for them or they are not ready for can strain relationships and stall their progress. Healing is not linear; people naturally move between daily life, moments of joy, and the hard work of processing harm. Accepting this rhythm in others without trying to influence it allows space for their journey to unfold authentically.

Ultimately, each of us is responsible for our own emotional safety, boundaries and decisions. It is inevitable that each choice we make affects our social systems, prompting reactions and adjustments from others. That can not be helped, and we can not use that as our guide.

Instead of trying to manage the feelings or manipulating others to react the way we think is best, if we focus on what resonates and feels right in our own healing, take responsibility only for our boundaries and behavior, doing our part will be easier. We can trust the social systems around us to adapt over time to our improving internal world in increasingly positive ways.

5. **Planning Family Events**
   When planning family gatherings intended for lightness, connection, or celebration, it's important to consider the needs of the most vulnerable individuals. Reach out to them in advance to understand how best to support them, ensuring they feel included while respecting their choice to avoid potentially distressing situations. Ask directly what would help them feel comfortable and supported if they choose to attend.

   For some, having a say in the dynamics, creating a safety plan, or deciding not to attend can make a significant difference. Every situation is unique, but open communication and genuine awareness help prevent gatherings from becoming another source of harm for our loved ones.

6. **Maintain a Balance Between Healing and Living**
   For families, it's important to find a balance between making space for healing and embracing life. Healing and living are not sequential. They coexist. Healing is a lifelong journey that takes significant energy, but daily life still needs to be lived.

   Everyone, including the GREEN, will continue to laugh, love, work, celebrate, tackle everyday tasks, and enjoy moments of lightness. These changing moods and actions do not mean the healing is complete. They are natural pauses that make the hard work of healing sustainable.

   Family members often say, "I thought they [the GREEN] were over it. It happened so long ago, and they seemed happy. They've been coming for the holidays, just got a promotion, and we had such a great time at the lake this summer." While joyful moments are an important part of life, they don't always reflect the full reality of what a GREEN might be experiencing.

   At the same time, family members can take the initiative to check in with the GREEN, acknowledge the impact of the harm, and express their ongoing support. These conversations, when approached with care and without judgment, can reaffirm connection and show a shared commitment to healing and growth.

Survivors often don't share how they are struggling. They might be genuinely caught up in the moment or they may not want to burden others with the truth of how they are really doing. Without being invited into a deeper and safer conversation, family members may not know what the GREEN is going through. The longer that topic goes without being raised, the more the wall between loved ones and the GREEN will become.

It is important for the GREEN to also remember that other family members are living their lives too. They need to work, play, keep up with their other relationships, take care of other loved ones and themselves. They can not be focused always on the harm event, and the survivor if they are going to be able to stay present when it really matters. They too need balance in their lives. When it seems they are stepping away from engaging in the healing journey, we can ask them without judgment how they are doing.

Everyone can strive to understand the rhythm of engaging in the intensity and then stepping back is natural. It doesn't necessarily signal indifference. We all have many aspects of our life to manage. So when we wonder what is happening with someone else, don't make up a story or build an answer from assumptions. Just ask.

7. **Rebuilding Trust in Relationships**
   Moving forward isn't about choosing between healing and maintaining family life. It is about finding a sustainable balance between the two. It can feel overwhelming to imagine repairing an entire family system, especially when trust has been broken. And, we don't usually rebuild trust system-wide; we do it one relationship at a time.

Each relationship is uniquely shaped by the two people involved. When larger family dynamics begin to fray, we return to the dyad; the individual connections that matter most to us. No one else can repair these bonds on our behalf. It's up to us to invest the time, energy, and care required to rebuild trust and co-create a new, healthier dynamic with each person we value. Every restored relationship strengthens the whole.

Not all relationships will return to what they once were. Some may need time and space. Others may never fully reconnect. It's not uncommon for individuals, especially the GREEN, to temporarily or permanently step back from the family system in order to integrate a reality that better aligns with their lived experience.

Taking space can help break old, unconscious patterns and create room for new ways of relating to emerge. Even when someone is doing strong internal work to change, coming back into the family dynamics can send them straight back to old coping mechanisms. A pause in connecting is often necessary to build the perspective and skills needed to return to the family system with more capacity to relate in the ways that serve us best.

In some cases, especially when family leaders are unwilling to acknowledge the harm, a more permanent distance may be needed. Even then, it's possible to remain in connection with those we care about by honoring their need for space without trying to fix or change it. Accepting the distance as the new normal, rather than something temporary or fighting against it, can allow the relationship to evolve on its own terms and rebuild trust in time.

Ultimately, we are each empowered to nurture the relationships that matter most to us. By relating to what is, rather than what we wish it were, and grieving what has been lost without resistance, we become more trustworthy in the eyes of others. This steady, respectful approach opens the door for deeper healing, even in the most challenging circumstances.

Unburdening Others

Sexual harm disrupts family dynamics in lasting ways. Survivors may feel responsible for protecting others' from the emotional burden of knowing what happened, siblings may keep up a façade of positivity and do their best to keep from causing any problems, and non-offending parents may neglect their own well-being by isolating themselves from their community, and insulating the family. In the midst of this, some will emerge as the emotional anchor, the caretaker.

The family caretaker listens, holds space, and tries to help everyone else navigate the minefield of emotions. They may adopt a fiercely independent or even anti-dependent mindset, meeting their own needs elsewhere to avoid burdening others. Their heightened vigilance leads them to anticipate and maneuver around potential triggers, which can be helpful initially but often becomes exhausting and unsustainable.

Over time, guilt may compel caretakers to keep stepping in for others, while resentment quietly builds. Unspoken expectations begin to emerge and those receiving the support may start to expect it. Gratitude can fall away, and while the caretaker keeps giving, burying the bad feeling, and the receiver keeps expecting to be prioritized, the relationship slowly erodes.

Our adult agency is disrupted when we do not take responsibility for ourselves. The more the caretaker anticipates the needs of others and does it for them, the more they undermine that person's self determination. The receiver may start to believe they can not take care of themselves, when stepping into their own adult power is exactly what brings momentum to the healing.

Healthy families don't rely on one emotional anchor. There are no rigid roles of "caretaker" and "care-receiver." In balanced adult relationships, care flows in both directions. Everyone gives and receives support according to their capacity, not out of obligation, but by choice.

We must embrace clear communication and compassionate boundaries. This means asking for help directly and accepting a "no" without judgment or anger. It means offering support only when we have the capacity to do so without feeling resentful and saying "no" when we can not, without spiraling into guilt. When support is requested without expectation, and offered freely, with an open heart, then accepted with gratitude, the system moves toward balance.

aking responsibility for our own well-being and decision making is foundational to healing. No one should be expected to care for another potentially capable adult, or carry the emotional weight for the entire family. When each person is empowered to care for themselves and support others from a place of balance, the system becomes more resilient.

Healing is a shared responsibility. While survivors need and deserve care, focusing all attention on one person can create new pressures and distort the path to recovery. True healing emerges when each member of the family sees themselves as both deserving of support and capable of offering it. This is what creates a sustainable, healing environment for everyone involved.

To maintain balance, it's important to both give and receive care. No single person should bear the full responsibility for family healing, nor should anyone be solely defined as the one who needs help and the one who should give it. Overzealous efforts to "help" can unintentionally weaken others' sense of agency, conveying the harmful message that they are incapable of healing on their own.

This balance applies to everyone touched by sexual harm. The survivors, offenders, non-offending parents, and other loved ones who frequently are relegated to the role of caretaker. While we cannot demand support from those unwilling or unable to provide it, we are also not obligated to give more than we can personally sustain. Expanding our support networks, both within and outside the family, ensures no one is overburdened and everyone has the space they need to heal. By actively seeking diverse sources of support and prioritizing our own healing journey, we reduce the risk of burnout and promote resilience. This approach fosters a healthier balance of care within the family system. Remember, prioritizing your own needs isn't selfish. It's a vital part of healing that benefits everyone.

The Holder of Rage

Anger is a natural and appropriate response to child sexual abuse, and has its place in the healing process. When a family member expresses outrage about the injustice of sexual harm, it can provide solace to the survivor, affirming they are not the only one suffering.

When anger turns destructive or vengeful, it can hinder healing for everyone involved. If one person's rage becomes overwhelming, it can cause others to withdraw, walk on eggshells, or avoid difficult conversations. This imbalance can lead to avoidance, secret-keeping, or emotional distance, stalling collective progress.

Distinguishing between anger that heals and anger that harms is important. Intense anger toward the abuser or those who failed to protect the child is valid. However, when it is too much, we might see the GREEN will even take their side in defense of their humanity. Remembering that engaging in a well managed anger lends itself to healing, and when it overwhelms others, it shuts down the process.

When channeled constructively, anger can be an impressive reformer. The one not afraid to embody their anger is often the one who wields significant influence. They have the power to break silences, demanding confrontation and accountability. Anger can provide the strength to voice difficult truths and set protective boundaries, especially when others feel unable to.

Constructive anger doesn't mean unleashing rage without restraint.

While expressing anger can be cathartic, it's important to avoid using it destructively. When anger is acted upon impulsively, we risk obscuring the real source of harm and perpetuating cycles of victimhood.

Instead, we focus on the natural consequences of direct or indirect harm. These involve setting healthy boundaries to protect ourselves and others, which often means limitations on those who are not containing themselves in ways that make others feel secure, understood, valued. In contrast, retribution seeks to inflict harm, which only deepens the collective trauma.

Constructive anger can be expressed in emotionally intense ways, but focuses on the impact someone's behavior had on us, and does not serve as a character assassination. When we choose to attack another, they will most likely become defensive and will not take into consideration the damage they have done. When we express ourselves from the "here is how my life has changed…" we have the potential for the other person to hear what we have said, take it in and feel the pain they have caused.

The Mediator

In many families, there's someone others naturally turn to when things get tense. Someone who listens well, stays grounded, and knows how to make people feel heard. This person often becomes the unofficial mediator: the one who keeps the peace, helps others navigate conflict, and works to maintain connection.

When harm has shaken the family system, this role can become even more central. People may look to the mediator to step in, smooth things over, or figure out how to make things right. Done thoughtfully, this can be a real gift to the family. A strong mediator doesn't carry the burden of fixing it. They help others bring their feelings to the right place and encourage them to work it through.

Instead of absorbing conflict, effective mediators coach others to speak directly, set clear boundaries, and avoid the triangulation of talking about someone rather than to them. Nothing undermines family trust like venting behind someone's back while avoiding an honest conversation. Encouraging open, direct communication when people are ready is one of the most powerful things a mediator can do.

Sometimes, mediators are also the ones who can pull people together for a needed conversation. In group conversations, establishing guidelines to keep communication respectful can give each person a chance to share their inner world, and listen to that of others. Mediators don't force perspective on others. They ask powerful questions that invoke thoughtful responses. This can be a turning point in conflict when done well.

That said, being the "go-to" person can be exhausting. Mediators within a family system are also impacted by the harm, and have their own feelings and coping mechanisms. The person assigned 'mediator' is not responsible for fixing everything, and is allowed to step back when it is too much.

This role isn't meant to be a lifelong assignment. It is just a part some of us may take on temporarily or during specific moments. When held too tightly or for too long, it can lead to burnout. When the responsibility of bringing people together is shared, it strengthens the family as a whole.

No Fixed Identities, Only Fluid Roles

To heal together, we must learn to balance our own needs *alongside* the needs of others. This balance must be allowed to ebb and flow to fundamentally shift how we relate to one another. It is a new day when we all must pull together in a different way to heal from harm.

The roles we take on in a healing family should be flexible and responsive, not fixed. When we lock ourselves into a single archetype, we reinforce a false narrative. The sense that one of us is strong enough to take care of the rest, while the others wait to be told what to do, hinders what is needed for each adult to find their footing. Leaders come

in different forms, and we all need support to get through this.
A healthier approach recognizes that every family member will struggle at times, and that each of us has the capacity to offer support in our own way. We do not need to show up for others the way they want, or the way someone else does. We lean into our own gifts, demeanor and ways of supporting others.

When we naturally feel most comfortable leading, we can practice the vulnerability of asking for help. When we're used to standing back and letting others take over, we look for ways to step up. This give-and-take builds resilience within the family system and strengthens trust. And trust is what is needed.

CHAPTER 22

Collective Healing

Everything that has ever happened to us shapes how we move through the world. It influences how we see ourselves, how we relate to others, and how we build community. Every action, every word, every silence reverberates through our relationships, often in ways we will never fully see.

Hurt vs. Harm

Not every painful experience leaves a permanent mark. Hurt may sting, but it doesn't necessarily shift the way we see the world. We have our ways of recovering and we will be fine relatively quickly. Harm, by contrast, reshapes us. It overwhelms our coping mechanisms, forcing us to build new ones. It alters our ability to trust, our sense of safety, our identity. While hurt may change how we feel about a person, harm changes how we move through the world.

What counts as harm isn't about the act itself, but the impact. The same experience can affect two people differently. One may recover quickly; another may carry it for life. This is why we must stop measuring harm by comparison and start listening for its unique imprint on a particular individual.

Unique Impact, Shared System

Harm may happen to an individual, but its effects are never contained there. The aftermath of harm changes the person and then the dynamics within families, communities, even generations. A betrayal between two people might quietly unravel friendships, isolate partners, disrupt children, and fracture extended relationships in subtle but lasting ways.

Systems absorb harm and hold onto it. Long after the original event, harm continues to echo through relationships. People who have been harmed may, in turn, harm others. Mistrust hardens. Roles become rigid. Behaviors that once served as protection turn into patterns of disconnection. Over time, the system begins to loop back on itself, replaying the original wound in new forms.

Unless we step back and learn to see the whole, we risk focusing only on the surface. Who's angry, who's withdrawn, who's difficult, while missing the deeper injury that binds them all. Healing must begin not only by naming what happened, but by tracing how it continues to live in the system.

The Protective Phase

When harm occurs, we instinctively protect ourselves. We shut down, pull away, get defensive, or over-function to avoid further pain. These protective behaviors may feel necessary, but they often block the very connection we need to heal.

Over time, protection becomes identity. We tell ourselves stories to justify distance: I can't trust anyone. No one really cares. I am better off on my own. And while these narratives may offer temporary safety, they also entrench isolation. The longer we stay in protection, the harder it becomes to let others in, even those trying to reach us.

Two Healing Paths

Healing from harm and healing from causing harm require different energy.

If we've been harmed, healing is an activation. It is the reclaiming of power and the rise of self-worth. It means letting go of the belief that what happened to us defines our value. It requires anger, not to destroy, but to fuel our return to self. Healing in this way is not passive. It's an active decision to stand tall again.

If we've caused harm, healing is a deactivation. It is a softening of defenses and a surrender to humility. Instead of explaining, we listen. Instead of justifying, we take responsibility. It's about making space for someone else's truth, even when it's hard to hear. This kind of healing asks us not to be let off the hook, but to stay in the discomfort long enough to grow.

One path rises up, the other quiets down. Both require courage. Both will transform the system.

The Individual and the Collective

Healing begins with the individual. Each of us must examine how we've been shaped by harm, both the harm done to us and the harm we may have caused. Without this personal reckoning, collective healing is impossible. Families that attempt to heal without individual inner work often retraumatize each other, bringing fear, pain, and confusion into the room without knowing how to hold it.

When one person begins to heal, the entire system feels the shift. Their growth may not immediately change others, but it changes the dynamic. At first, it might even bring more conflict or disruption, as their clarity challenges the status quo. But this is part of the healing process.

We cannot carry on with business as usual once someone starts to do the deep work. That person's boundaries begin to restore balance. Their truth-telling creates space. And their compassion, even in discomfort, can begin to soften the defensiveness around them.

I once knew a man who, after being betrayed by a close friend, spent decades in emotional retreat. What started as one betrayal grew into a belief: Men can't be trusted. His wife, children, and remaining friends tried for years to reach him, but he kept the door closed. As he remained at home, so did his wife. Their children stopped visiting as much. The depression and resentment grew worse. Over time, they stopped trying to reach him.

Imagine if he had chosen to heal. If, instead of clinging to bitterness, he had recognized how his response deepened his own pain and hurt his family. What if he had reconnected with those he did trust, accepted that he couldn't change the one who betrayed him, and stopped waiting for an apology that would never come? His healing might have opened new space in his life. He might have stumbled across the nuance that all men are not the same. Some can be trusted.

What a relief for his wife and children to have him opening his heart again. Maybe he could finally see how hard his depression and isolation had been on their lives. Maybe even drawing his old friend toward accountability. Or perhaps not. But either way, he would have reclaimed the life that harm once stole.

What if his wife had healed first? What if, while he remained closed off, she chose to stop carrying his loneliness and started living her own life. She started to travel with her friends again, building new friendships, finding joy again. At first, he might have felt abandoned. But maybe, just maybe, seeing her shift softened something in him. Maybe it stirred the possibility of change.

This is how healing moves through a system. Not by pressuring someone to change, or trying to convince them to see it a different way, but through leading by example. Not through waiting for someone who is stuck, but through choosing to heal and continue living, inviting them to join in. One person's healing shifts the emotional gravity. And those still in their protective stance may eventually begin to thaw.

The Choice Before Us

Collective healing is not about getting everyone to agree, feel the same, or arrive at some fictitious destination at the same time. It's about each of us doing our part in caring for our own growth while holding space for others to do the same, if and when they are ready.

We must let go of the idea that others need to change before we can feel peace. They don't need to meet our needs. They just need to be who they are, and we will choose how close we remain to them. The natural consequence of not doing our healing work is feeling less close to others. And humans need others, so it might motivate some change.

This work is not about rescuing someone in the system so that we feel better. It's about participation. Each step we take toward honesty, toward repair, toward integrity adds weight to a different kind of future. One where connection is earned, not forced. One where safety is created, not demanded. One where those who want to heal, can.

This is our greatest responsibility, and our greatest opportunity: to break the cycle, to leave a different legacy, and to move the world forward.

See inside back cover for an expanded version of:
The Path to Healing from Harm.

CHAPTER 23

Our Inescapable Interconnectedness

Living in *Right Relationship* means aligning our actions and intentions in harmony with those around us. This concept, while simple, carries profound implications. It reminds us that our interactions are interconnected, shaping the environment we live in and reflecting back what we contribute. When we act with compassion, we invite compassion. When we act defensively or aggressively, we foster distrust and hostility.

Being in alignment with ourselves, others, and our environment requires a heightened awareness. It calls for a deliberate and mindful approach, one that invites us to take responsibility for how we are impacting the world around us. This isn't about perfection or moral superiority; it's about generating a feedback loop. When we care about our own needs and the needs of others, it becomes a self-generating field of respect and mutual support.

Our choices, when born out of fear, or unresolved harm can perpetuate the dynamics we hope to avoid. In our pursuit of security at any cost, we may create environments that become increasingly more alienating. Disconnection pushes us all into an increased vigilant and defensive state, where empathy diminishes and self-preservation takes over.

From this place, we begin to see the world as hostile. We seek power, control, and resources to protect ourselves, often without regard for how that impacts others. In turn, others experience us as threatening and respond in kind, seeking their own power and control to stay safe. The result is a self-perpetuating cycle of fear, distortion, and harm.

Right Relationship offers a way out of this cycle. It taps into the wellspring of our intrinsic worth, which is neither enhanced by our achievements nor diminished by our mistakes. Recognizing our own humanity allows us to more readily see it in others, fostering trust and mutual respect.

Sexual harm does not occur in isolation; it has reverberated through families and communities for generations, affecting everyone in both visible and unseen ways. The harm endured by countless children who then grew into adults carrying unhealed pain, has too often led to more harm, both to themselves and others. This cycle continues today.

The task of creating a world free from sexual harm can feel overwhelming. It becomes more manageable when we focus on what we *can* control: our own actions. When we align with one another, we contribute to a collective effort to restore balance. A world where children are safe from sexual harm is not a fantasy. It is the highest expression of the natural order.

Our interconnectedness is inescapable. Every choice we make ripples outward, shaping lives in ways we may never fully see. The truth is, healing doesn't wait for the perfect moment or the right person to start—it begins with us.

We all want a future where children are safe, families are whole, and communities are grounded in care. But that future won't appear on its own. It is built, choice by choice, conversation by conversation, by people brave enough to break old patterns and live with intention.

Young people are the future unfolding before us. With our support and their vision, they have the power to lead us into a world where harm is not passed down, where safety is woven into the fabric of everyday life. This future isn't promised—it's created. And it becomes possible when we choose to do the work, hold one another with care, and stay the course.

It becomes possible only when we agree to **healing together**.

PART VI

EPILOGUE

CHAPTER 24

Managing the Crisis as the Adult Leader

Practical Guidance for Families in Crisis

This chapter is for families in the first wave of crisis—those who have just learned that sexual harm has occurred within the family. While the rest of this book focuses on healing after the immediate threat has passed, I know that many readers may be turning to these pages in the earliest moments of impact.

You may have just discovered that a child has been harmed and are scrambling to figure out what to do next. Or perhaps the harm happened long ago, but the disclosure is new, and you're facing the shock of navigating this truth between adults who are all still very much part of each other's lives.

If you're not yet in a place to think about healing because the harm is still unfolding, the dynamics are still volatile, or the next steps feel overwhelming, this chapter is for you. What follows is not about processing the past, but about stabilizing the present. These early steps are meant to help you create safety, reduce chaos, and begin to respond in ways that protect everyone involved, especially those most vulnerable.

Every family's situation is different. There are no perfect scripts. But there are steadying practices, and even in the midst of crisis, there are choices that can lay the groundwork for future healing.

1. Establish Immediate Safety

Physical Safety:

The top priority will always be ensuring the safety of any young person or children who may be at risk. If there's an immediate danger or the possibility of continued harm, take decisive action. This could include:

- **Supervising interactions between children.**
- **Creating secure sleeping arrangements.**
- **Preventing the offender from having access to vulnerable individuals.**
- **Engage the authorities where appropriate.**

If the offender is an adult, it is not enough for them to promise not to cause further harm to a child or children. They must seek treatment and lose all access to children immediately.

Emotional Safety:

Emotional safety matters as much as physical safety. Shield the harmed child from exposure to the offender or triggering environments. Communicate openly about the steps being taken to protect them and ensure they feel heard and supported.

2. Responding to Sibling Abuse

For Younger Children:

When harm occurs between siblings, prioritize professional support from therapists trained in problematic sexual behaviors in minors. Actions to take include:

- **Take seriously the need to create safety in the home.**
- **Set clear and consistent boundaries in the home.**
- **Supervise the child who caused harm around other children.**
- **Seek professional support for both.**
- **Engage children in age-appropriate conversations about what happened.**
- **Continue conversations with both siblings over time.**

By framing this as an adult responsibility, we reduce the emotional burden on the children and model accountability. It is not enough to tell the child that their behavior was 'not ok' or to punish them in some way. Telling them not to do it again is not enough intervention to ensure safety. Families often need professional support to find out why this behavior occurred, and guidance for what to do next. If managed well, there is a good chance that the impact could be lessened considerably.

For Older or Adult Siblings:

When the harm is disclosed later, focus on emotional safety:

- **Believe the disclosure without questioning or challenging the details.**
- **Avoid immediate fact-finding or confrontations.**
- **Support each sibling in setting and honoring their own boundaries.**

3. Managing Disclosures About an Adult Offender

Protecting Children:
If the harm was caused by a parent, grandparent, or other adult caretaker or relative, take immediate steps to ensure they no longer pose a risk to children. This may include:

- **Communicating with other family members to create a safety network.**
- **Preventing the offender's access to all young people.**
- **Involving the authorities where appropriate.**

Respecting the Survivor's Boundaries:
Never force a survivor to interact with the offender. Survivors should have complete agency over their level of contact, if any. Establish this as a firm boundary early on to prevent further emotional harm.

In situations where the person who caused harm remains in the home, is unwilling to leave, and the family lacks the resources to separate, it is critical to prioritize the child's safety—both physical and emotional. Give the child as much agency as is age-appropriate, and create protective structures that minimize the risk of further harm.

While many families choose not to involve child protection services—a decision that is often rooted in fear, mistrust, or concern about unintended consequences—this choice comes with serious responsibility. It is not enough to simply ask the person who caused harm to stop. If the adults in the home cannot ensure the child's ongoing safety, outside intervention may be necessary, despite the complications it can bring.

4. Balancing Family Dynamics and Boundaries

Honoring the Survivor's Needs:
If the adult survivor requests the family to cut ties with the offender, approach this request with understanding. This often stems from a need for security and validation.

Supporting the Offender's Accountability:
Maintaining some connection with the offender, as in the case of sibling abuse or other circumstances when appropriate, can support their journey toward accountability and growth.

Clear Communication:
Be transparent with the survivor about your choices. While you may choose to maintain a connection with the offender, make it clear that this does not diminish the seriousness of their actions. Commit to not prioritizing the needs of the offender over the survivor's physical or emotional safety.

5. Engaging with Child Protective Services or Legal Systems

While most families choose not to involve child protective services or law enforcement, there are situations where it can be an important call to make. Particularly when a child remains at immediate risk, and there is no family member who has the power to keep them safe or when the offender is likely to harm again. Calling in a case to the police or child protective services is not always going to result in action, nor does it come without its own consequence. This is something to consider, and you can always call to talk to them before reporting a situation.

- **Understand the limitations of the system.**
- **Even when a family reports the harm and the authorities intervene, it does not ensure that the case will have enough**

evidence to proceed.

- **Be aware of secondary trauma when engaging with the legal system.**
- **Build a trusted network of safe adults to protect the child regardless of the outcome of reporting.**
- **Make informed decisions based on the specific needs of your family.**

6. Addressing Intergenerational Patterns of Harm

Breaking cycles of intergenerational harm begins with open communication. The best way to keep child sexual abuse from happening again is to talk openly about what it is, how it impacts others, and how to heal from it.

- **Normalize conversations about the family history of sexual harm and teach the adults in your child's life about safety from sexual harm.**
- **Encourage younger generations to prioritize speaking openly with their children, staying vigilant in age appropriate ways and take proactive measures for prevention.**
- **Discuss protocols for child protection with external caregivers, such as schools or camps.**

7. Confronting the Offender

When an adult leader becomes aware of the harm, and the offending party has not been confronted, especially if they remain active in the family system, they should be confronted.

- **The child should not be present when an adult confronts the offender.**

- **Respect the adult survivor's wishes and readiness to address the harm and confront the offender, unless that offender is at risk of harming another child.**
- **Ensure the confrontation prioritizes safety and accountability over retaliation.**

8. Navigating Relationships with the Offender

If you choose to maintain a connection with the offender:

- **Set unwavering boundaries to protect all children from the potential of new harm events.**
- **Support the offenders efforts toward recovery and accountability without excusing their actions.**
- **Insist the offender be the one to take responsibility for their own recovery and repair.**
- **Respect the survivor's decision if they choose to distance themselves from anyone who maintains a relationship with the offender.**

9. Supporting Adult Survivors Who Disconnect

When a survivor chooses to distance themselves from the family:

- **Respect their need for space without trying to convince them otherwise.**
- **Maintain a non-intrusive line of communication when possible.**
- **Balance patience with sincere efforts to keep the relationship open.**
- **Do not advocate for the survivor to see it another way or repeatedly ask them to be responsible for someone else's grief.**

- **Stay away from transactional requests, such as "if we pay for a new car, will you come to Thanksgiving?" or "if you pay for a new car, I will come to Thanksgiving."**
- **Recognize things have changed, and all we can do is get the support we need to start our own healing.**

10. Creating a Circle of Safety Within the Family

Real change often begins with a small, committed group of individuals inside the family. When two or more come together to do the work of healing, family dynamics start to change.

- **Partner with another adult who shares your commitment to addressing the harm.**
- **Create a foundation of safety and accountability that can serve as a model for others in the family.**
- **Focus on leading by example, rather than trying to coerce change.**

Final Thoughts

In the early stages of a crisis or disclosure, it is natural to feel overwhelmed. By focusing on immediate safety, respecting boundaries, and taking deliberate steps, you can help stabilize your family. Healing is a long journey that comes well after the crisis has passed. It takes time. There is no need to make permanent decisions about relationships while trying to bring about physical and emotional stability. Work in the present, and the rest will come when it can.

CHAPTER 25

A Word on Prevention

While this book has focused on how to respond to harm and how to stop that harm from rippling through relationships for years to come—it's also worth pausing to consider how we prevent sexual harm from happening in the first place.

This isn't an exhaustive guide to prevention, but rather a starting point. It is a brief list of ideas to start thinking differently about safety, responsibility, and culture. Real prevention goes beyond good intentions and downloading statistics. It requires skills that most of us weren't taught: how to recognize boundary crossings early, how to talk openly with children and other adults about sexual harm, how to ask the right questions of caregivers, and how to respond skillfully when someone discloses harm.

These are not instincts. They are learned behaviors. And they take time and practice to develop. If prevention is something you're ready to engage with more deeply, the next step is to seek out interactive, skills-based training where you can learn, practice, and build the confidence to act when it matters most.

What follows are just a few things to consider as you begin to shift your lens from reacting to actively preventing. Small changes in awareness can have a powerful impact over time.

Consider these three types of families when thinking about prevention:

1. **Unaware Families**
   These families have little or no awareness of child sexual abuse. The adults may find it difficult to imagine that someone they know, especially within their own family, could harm a child in this way. To them, sexual abuse feels like a distant issue, something that happens "somewhere else," far removed from their own lives and communities.

2. **Concerned but Passive Families**
   These families may have some understanding or experience with child sexual abuse, often through stories they've heard or their own unspoken or unresolved trauma. While they are concerned about the possibility of harm, they don't take active steps to prevent it. Instead, they hope their children will remain safe, which can lead to missed warning signs or hesitation when decisive action is needed.

3. **Proactive Families**
   Proactive families are led by adults who are well-informed about the risks and signs of child sexual abuse. These adults recognize that awareness and communication are key. They talk openly about the topic and create an environment where children feel empowered to express themselves. Proactive families educate their children about their bodies in a positive, shame-free way, teaching them to recognize discomfort, voice their feelings, and understand their right to bodily autonomy and consent.

Understanding these categories underscores the importance of moving toward a proactive approach. By staying informed and fostering open dialogue, families can create safer environments for their children. By educating ourselves, we feel more able to set appropriate boundaries and speak up if something feels wrong.

Engage in Inner Work:

Begin by examining your own internal barriers and biases. This requires confronting uncomfortable truths and recognizing any assumptions that might prevent you from addressing signs of potential sexual harm. Personal introspection builds the clarity and courage needed to respond to abuse effectively.

Foster Open Dialogue:

Create environments where talking about child sexual abuse is normalized. This means discussing the issue openly at home, in schools, and within community groups. Open discussions reduce stigma, empower children and adults to voice concerns, and create a culture where seeking support is safe and encouraged.

Recognize Warning Signs:

Learn to identify the signs that a child may be experiencing abuse, such as behavioral changes, emotional distress, or physical symptoms. Approach these signs calmly and seek to understand the child's experience without judgment or raising the alarms. Recognize that children may struggle to articulate what is happening, so we may need to ask questions to fully understand. By building trust and keeping the lines of communication open, the child or young person may feel safe enough to disclose more and accept your help.

Prioritize Child Safety:

Always make decisions based on what is safest for the child, even if it means confronting uncomfortable truths or challenging family norms. Carefully consider who has access to your child, and build relationships with other adults to establish a safety network. Make it clear to everyone that discussing child sexual abuse openly is something you feel comfortable doing, which will reduce the risk that your child will be targeted.

Identify Red Flag Behaviors:

Be alert to signs of grooming behavior, such as boundary testing, excessive attention, or manipulative tactics designed to gain a child's trust. Address these behaviors early, even when it's uncomfortable. Remember that grooming can also target the adults in a family. Offenders may work to earn your trust before harming a child. Stay vigilant and willing to discuss sexual abuse and safety with anyone in contact with your child.

Address Boundary Crossings:

If you notice someone testing or crossing physical boundaries, intervene firmly and compassionately. Set clear limits and communicate expectations. Many offenders start by eroding physical boundaries through seemingly innocent acts like tickling or unwanted hugs. Be proactive in establishing consent and reinforcing appropriate boundaries to prevent escalation.

Act Decisively in Harmful Situations:

If harm is occurring or has occurred, take immediate action to ensure safety. This could mean removing the child from the situation, contacting authorities, or organizing a network of trusted adults to provide ongoing protection. Ensuring safety requires decisive, informed steps and a community of allies.

Handle Disclosures with Sensitivity:

When a child shares they have been harmed, prioritize their emotional well-being. Validate their bravery and reassure them that they did nothing wrong. Avoid pressing them for unnecessary details; instead, provide emotional support and reassurance that you will keep them safe. Your response sets the foundation for their healing and can influence their willingness to seek further help.

Support the Offender in Seeking Recovery:

If someone in your life shows signs of being attracted to children but has not acted on it, engage in a direct but compassionate conversation. Let them know support is available to prevent harm. If someone has already caused harm, encourage them to seek professional help. Providing resources can aid in their rehabilitation, but always prioritize safety alongside any efforts to support change.

Instill Hope and Healing:

We can heal from anything. To all survivors of harm, we empathize, and instill hope that the more they speak about it, the more the shame will transfer to the one who caused the harm. Let them know they are not alone, and you will support them throughout.

Ongoing Conversations:

Healing is not a one-time conversation. It requires consistent, ongoing dialogue to maintain momentum. As family leaders, take responsibility for creating opportunities to revisit the topic, fostering progress and sustaining a safe, open environment. By implementing these steps, we can create safer environments for our children and contribute to the broader effort of preventing and ending child sexual abuse in our family and communities.

Be Part of the Movement

If this book has been meaningful to you, please join us in reshaping how our society addresses child sexual abuse. Hidden Water is the only nonprofit of its kind, providing a unique, community-based, restorative approach to healing from sexual harm.

Built by families, for families, Hidden Water provides free, globally accessible online services, creating a safe space for those seeking meaningful healing and repair. Through this growing community, we bring people together to move from isolation to connection with others who have had a similar experience in their family systems.

By supporting Hidden Water, you can directly increase our capacity to serve more families and expand the reach of this life-changing work.

Donate Here:
www.hiddenwatercircle.org/we-heal-together

Thank you for your support in this groundbreaking work.

Elizabeth Clemants
Founder and Executive Director, Hidden Water
www.hiddenwatercircle.org

ACKNOWLEDGMENTS

First and foremost, I want to thank my husband, **Glen Parker**, for the countless hours, weeks, months, and years he devoted to editing the many drafts of this book. His evenings, weekends, and even vacations spent tirelessly marking up pages were matched only by the emotional support he provided throughout this ten-year process. Without his love, encouragement, and belief in my ability to finish, this book would not have come to fruition.

My deepest gratitude goes to **Taylor Yess**, whose unwavering work ethic, exceptional competence, and dedication kept Hidden Water afloat during very challenging times. From the very beginning of this book, Taylor's encouragement, insight, and trust in this idea, and in the organization have been a solid foundation for me to rely on. None of this would have been possible without her steadfast presence.

Thank you to the Hidden Water Keepers and Participants. Everything I know, I learned from sitting in circle with you all. To **Laurent**, **RK**, and **Anne-Marie**—the Purple, Orange, and Blue leaders—thank you for generously sharing your insights and providing feedback for this book. Your wisdom has enriched this work in ways words cannot fully convey.

Chez Bryan Ong @spoonandforkstudio.com, the aesthetic creativity behind preparing this book to manifest itself in the world. Your seemingly endless patience with me does not go unnoticed, and I am deeply grateful.

Finally, I want to honor **My Children**. Thank you for your patience and understanding during my absences and for forgiving my inability to pick up the phone when you called. I was working to bring forth my life's work. I hope you are proud to be living proof that intergenerational child sexual abuse can end. You three are my greatest accomplishment, and seeing you thrive brings me endless joy.

To everyone who brought the collective wisdom, whether directly or indirectly, thank you.

Grateful and Blessed,
Elizabeth

Elizabeth Clemants is the Founder and Executive Director of Hidden Water, a restorative justice initiative focused on individual and family healing from sexual harm. She brings a unique blend of expertise to this work, drawing from her experiences as a social worker, court/community mediator, and a practitioner of northern shamanic traditions. With decades of experience in individual and family work, Elizabeth has integrated these diverse disciplines to create a groundbreaking approach. This innovative intervention fosters profound individual healing, which opens the door to relational repair, and conflict resolution within family systems affected by past sexual harm.

Elizabeth has a Bachelor's in Social Work from Iowa State University ('93). Upon returning from the Peace Corps ('93-'96), she moved to New York City and earned a Master's in Social Work with a Minor in Law from Columbia University ('98). Elizabeth has dedicated her career to conflict resolution, teaching and healing. She opened her private practice, Planning Change, in 2004 where she continues to work with individuals, families, and organizations. She has been an adjunct professor at Fordham Law School since 2005, and a conflict resolution trainer for the New York State Unified Court System since 2000.

Elizabeth was born and raised in Edina, MN, USA, and still considers herself a Minnesotan. She lives happily in Brooklyn, NY, with her husband, three children, and one big dog. Many Sundays they can be found cheering for the MN Vikings to finally win the Super Bowl.